A 2024 Starting-Point Guide

Gothenburg, Sweden

Plus, the Västra Götaland Region

Barry Sanders – writing as:

B G Preston

Gothenburg, Sweden

ISBN: 9798858079149

3rd Edition -Updated April2024-AR

Acknowledgements: The author greatly appreciates Sandra Sanders' contributions. She provided substantial editorial assistance and took several of the photographs included in this work.

Photography: Maps and photographs in the Starting-Point Guides are a mixture of those taken by the author and other resources including Shutterstock, Adobe Media, Wikimedia, Google Earth, and Google Maps. No photograph in this work should be used without checking with the author first.

Gothenburg / Göteborg
The ideal stress-free small city

Contents

Preface & Some Travel Suggestions

The central focus or "starting point" of this guide is **Gothenburg, Sweden** and much of the neighboring region known as **Västra Götaland**.

This is not a complete guide to the entire Swedish west coast or every attraction within the region. Such a guide would go beyond the suggested scope of staying in one town and having enjoyable and relaxing day trips from there.

Each of us has varying preferences and what we look for when visiting a new area can differ dramatically. This guide's focus is on orienting you to Gothenburg and providing highlights on the layout of the town and area and its leading attractions.

This is not an in-depth guide which details every aspect of the history or background of each point of interest. This guide's goal is to ensure you have a better understanding and high-level view of such aspects as: getting around in town, where the sights are, areas to consider lodging and some highlights near town.

The Ideal Itinerary:

The First Suggestion: If your travel schedule allows plan on staying at least 2 nights in Gothenburg and ideally 3 or 4 nights.

This is an area with a wonderful variety of sights outside of town, especially if you enjoy nature and participating in outdoor activities. Several days are needed to obtain even a moderate understanding of what this area has to offer.

The Second Suggestion: Leave one day open and unplanned near the end of your stay. Build in a day in which you have not pre-booked any excursions or planned major activities.

The reason for this is, once there, you will discover places which you either want to revisit or learn of new places which appeal to you. If you have a full schedule, you will lose this luxury.

What if you only have one full day here?
Consider one of the three general approaches:

1 – City Focus: Stay in central Gothenburg and simply explore the town and the canals. The main attraction here is this beautiful city so get to know it well. Head over to the historic Haga district for lunch or walk the Avenyn to do some shopping. This is an easy town to explore on foot or take one of the Hop-On Tour buses.

2 – Island Fun & a Bit of Town: Close to Gothenburg is a beautiful island archipelago. Take a ferry out to the islands and do some exploring. Then come back into town and spend the rest of the day exploring central Gothenburg.

3 – Auto Experiences: If you are in town to pick up your new Volvo, follow the guidelines of the Volvo trip planners. They are well experienced in guiding you in exploring the area. Or, if you are not picking up a car, consider taking a Volvo factory tour and then combining this with some in town explorations.

Relax along one of the canals in the heart ot the city.

Consider a City Pass:

When staying in a city filled with attractions, purchasing **a** Gothenburg Go City Pass can be advantageous.

Acquire one if you are likely to visit multiple attractions. Do not acquire one if you only want to visit one or two attractions during your stay.

When visiting Gothenburg, you will have options of purchasing the Gothenburg Go City Pass[1] in increments of 1, 2, 3 or 5 days. See chapter 5 for details.

Websites for this pass are:

- www.GothenburgPass.com or
- www.GoCity.com/Gothenburg

---

[1] Go City is a firm which provides similar passes to several cities across the globe such as: London, Paris, Stockholm, Vienna and many others.

Visit the Visitor Center:

Gothenburg's main tourist information office, the **Visitor Centre**, is conveniently located in the heart of the tourist area, near canals, many hotels and numerous restaurants.

Obtain information from this office on available tours and places to visit. Even if you have done substantial research prior to your trip, it is likely you will learn of opportunities which you had not previously discovered.

Before your trip, visit the Gothenburg Tourist Center website. Among the many helpful information elements is the ability to order a detailed Gothenburg City Guide with detailed maps. Having this map and guide with you prior to arriving in the city can be helpful. This map is a bit buried on the site so simply use the site's search box for "map" and the city guide tourist map will come up as an option.

Address: Kungsportspatsen 2, 411 10 Göteborg

Website: **www.Goteborg.com**

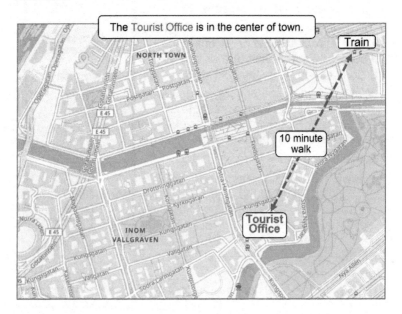

The Tourist Office is in the center of town.

Obtain Information on Local Transportation:

Most Scandinavian cities such as Gothenburg will have excellent tram and bus systems. In the case of Gothenburg, there are also water ferries to help you move across the river.

Understanding the transportation system during a first visit to a city can be daunting. The staff at the Visitor Centre will be able to provide help and perhaps sell you tickets to use during your stay. Chapter 4 provides additional guidance on the transportation network in Gothenburg. Also, check out the following list of apps. Several of them are very helpful in using this complete but complex network.

Gothenburg has an extensive tram system.
Photo Source: A. Otrebski - Wikimedia Commons

Using the area transportation is a fun way to get to know the city and understand how the locals live and travel. At the worst, you may head off to an unintended locale which can lead to exploring parts of the city you hadn't planned on. At a minimum you can count on viewing more of the town and its varied neighborhoods.

Download Some Apps:

With the incredible array of apps for Apple and Android de-vices, almost every detail you will need for a great trip is available up to and including where to find public toilets. The following are some suggested apps and a search through your online store will likely find additional helpful ones.

Gothenburg Area Apps:

- Västtrafic To Go: Gothenburg has a comprehensive and complex trans-portation system. This app shows routes and schedules to help you get around. Tickets and passes may be purchased directly from this app.

- Gothenburg Offline City Map: Very detailed maps of Gothenburg show-ing sights, shopping, restaurants.

- Gothenburg Map and Walks: De-veloped by GPSmyCity, a firm which does a great job in providing info on local attractions and suggested walks.

- Go City Pass: The Go City app for Gothenburg and other cities which provides discounts to area attractions and tours.

The Gothenburg Tram & Bus App

- Gothenburg Tram & Bus Map: Very helpful app to aid you in using local trams and buses.

- Botaniska Göteborg: Gothenburg has a large and impressive botanical garden. This app provides maps and guidance on what you may find here.

- Next Bike: This city has an excellent bike share service and the company providing the bikes is Styr & Ställ. The Next Bike app provides details on where the bike share/rental stations are and if bikes are available.

Sweden Travel and Helpful Information:

- <u>SJ Trains in Sweden:</u> If you will be traveling by train through Sweden this app is highly recommended. It is provided by the Swedish rail system, and you may buy train tickets directly from this app.

- <u>Sweden Guide:</u> Helpful and historical information on many cities and attractions throughout Sweden.

General Travel Apps:[2]

- <u>Rome2Rio</u>: An excellent way to research all travel options including rental cars, trains, flying, ferries, and taxis. The app provides the ability to purchase tickets directly online.

- <u>Trip Advisor</u>: Probably the best overall app for finding details on most hotels, restaurants, excursions, and attractions.

- <u>Flush:</u> A very helpful app which provides guidance on where to find public or other available toilets.

The Rome2Rio app and website are great travel planning tools.

~ ~ ~ ~ ~ ~

---

[2] <u>General Travel Apps:</u> There are numerous excellent travel apps to select from. The ones cited here are recommended by the author, but your search for helpful apps should not be limited to this.

1: Gothenburg Introduction
The City with Two Names

Gothenburg or **Göteborg**[3] Which is the right name? These seemingly interchangeable names can be confusing. Either of these two spellings show up on various signs, websites or tour information.

As it turns out, this city actually has two official names and is the only city in Sweden to do this.

For most English-speakers, sticking with the name Gothenburg, will be fine and you don't need to feel embarrassed if you hear it pronounced differently. For simplicity, this guide will stick with the Gothenburg designation.

> Simply say…
>
> **"Got in burg"**
>
> Or for fun, you can use "G Burg"

A Bit About Gothenburg:

Gothenburg is Sweden's second largest city with a population of 580,000 population.[4] The metro area has roughly one million inhabitants. The size of this city is such that it is not overwhelming

---

[3] Göteborg pronunciation: It is not necessary to use this version of the name but if you want to give it a try: "Yeh ta bore e". And, yes, saying "Goth en burg" works too.

[4] Population data: Source, Wikipedia.

and is easy to navigate. It also has an enjoyable variety of attractions and every convenience you could want.

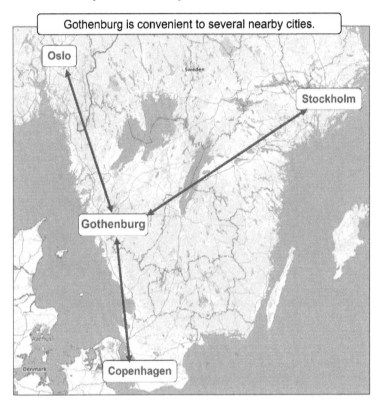

Gothenburg is convenient to several nearby cities.

Visitors to Gothenburg will find a delightful and easy city to explore on foot. (Unless you are mobility impaired). Most of central Gothenburg is fairly level, making walking easy. The star of the show is the town itself and its canals. Yes, there are several notable attractions and museums, but the town is a delight. It is not filled with major structures such as those you would find in Paris or London, it is, rather, a very clean city with clean air and many great areas to shop, dine and stroll. Just focusing your time on wandering along the canals and tree-lined lanes is a treat for most of us.

Gothenburg's center is active with broad streets & tram lines.

Another enjoyable aspect of central Gothenburg is that it is not overrun with tourists. The center of town is intended for local shopping and dining and does not cater specifically to tourism. Even areas such as the historic Haga district (See chapter 6) are filled with locals dining and partying. So, stroll a bit. Find a café for your first fika (Swedish coffee break), and just enjoy the air and the relaxing ambiance of this town.

Fika

The Skanskaskrapan Building
A modern office complex along the river in Gothenburg
Head to the cafe and lookout at the top for great views.
Photo Source: Arlid Vagen - Wikimedia Commons

This is the busiest seaport in Sweden and all Nordic countries. Roughly one-third of all international transportation in and out of Sweden goes through this port. This leads to an interesting aspect of Gothenburg and the area...water. The city's river and canal network define much of this beautiful city and greatly adds to the enjoyment of exploring the town.

If you arrive by ferry or cruise ship, the ports for these ships are within walking distance of town.

Gothenburg's canals outline much of the city.
Photo Source: Jonpet - Wikimedia Commons

Gothenburg has Sweden's busiest seaport.

The center of Gothenburg is a bit out from the main airport and the western shoreline with its many islands. The good news is there is excellent transportation, (see chapter 2) and these destinations are easy to reach.

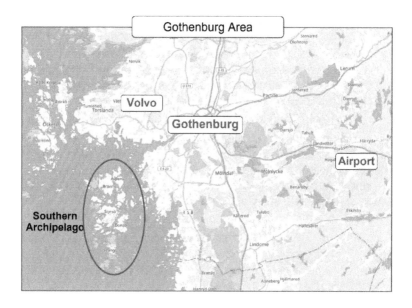

In addition to the pleasant streets and numerous shopping opportunities, the city and surrounding area are home to several important destinations including: (See chapters 6 & 7 for details)

- University: The large University of Gothenburg sits in the heart of town and has a population of over 30,000 students. With

The University of Gothenburg
Source: Natonato - Wikimedia Commons

so many university students living here, this leads to a very youthful feel.

- Volvo has its headquarters here along with large production facilities. Many individuals order their Volvos and come to Gothenburg to pick them up and have fun exploring the area before returning the vehicle to be shipped home.

- Lisenberg Amusement Park – sits just south of city center and is one of Sweden's largest amusement parks.

- Old Town / Haga: A delightful maze of narrow cobblestone streets with small cafes and shops. A short distance from the center of town but worth the effort to head here.

The central area of Gothenburg where most visitors tend to stay, shop and explore is compact and easy to find your way around. Most hotels and shops are in the area between the train station to the north and the university area to the south. One broad avenue, the Avenyn stretches south for several blocks and provides an enjoyable array of shops and restaurants.

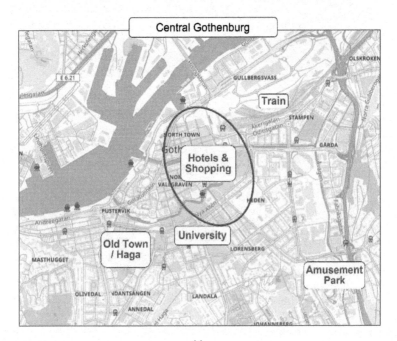

The Skansen Kronan Fortress
Overlooking the historic Haga district.
Photo Source: A. Fagerving - Wikimedia Commons

A Few Facts & Some History:

- Population: Gothenburg, or Göteborg is Sweden's second largest city and is about half of Stockholm's population which is a bit over 1.5 million.

- Nordic Country Size Rank: Gothenburg is the 5th largest city within the group of Nordic countries which include Denmark, Finland, Iceland, Norway and Sweden.

- 400th Anniversary: Gothenburg reached 400 years old in 2021.

- Västra Götaland: Gothenburg is the capital of Västra Götaland County. This county stretches north to Norway and east to the large Lake Vänern. You will often see the term **Västra Götaland** associated with Gothenburg. This is formally the name of the county where Gothenburg is situated, but it often refers to the whole region. This area stretches north to the Norway border, down along the coast a short distance and inland to encompass numerous towns and lakes of all sizes. It also covers thousands of islands along the coast.

- **Accolades:** This city was given the honor of "The world's most sustainable destination." It has received this honor for five years straight between 2016 and 2021.

- **Early Settlement:** When the city was built, it was influenced by the Dutch who were a political power at the time. One delightful result of this is the numerous canals which work their way through Gothenburg.

  Many of the early settlers were from Germany and Scotland who had been brought in by King Gustavus Adolphus in the 17th century. The goal had been to build a town at the mouth of the Göta älv River which would be large enough to sustain commerce to Sweden's west coast. Shortly after this, Swedish families moved in and soon outnumbered the early Dutch, German and Scottish settlers.

- **Stone Age Beginnings:** Prior to the formal start of Gothenburg in 1621, the city had been inhabited for thousands of years with archeological findings dating back to the Stone Age. Several ancient rock carvings which may be found here attest to this.

- **Industrialization:** Gothenburg really came into its own as an industrial city in the 19th century. Prior to this, in 1800 the population was only 13,000, but with the growth of industrialization it grew to 130,000 by the end of the 19th century. Before this time, the area's primary industry was fishing.

- **Few Historic Buildings Remain:** When the city was founded in the 17th century and before this time, most buildings were made of wood. Unfortunately, due to the ravages of time, very few of these wood structures remain. Most of the historical buildings here, such as Skansen Kronan fortress are all made of stone or brick.

- **Sports:** Gothenburg is the birthplace of football (soccer) in Sweden. There is a large stadium, (the Ullevi) near central Gothenburg which can seat over 70,000 fans. If you are lucky, a game may be scheduled for when you come here. Check www.Ullevi.se for details.

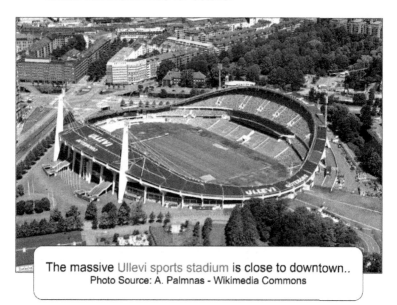

The massive Ullevi sports stadium is close to downtown..
Photo Source: A. Palmnas - Wikimedia Commons

Swedish Currency:

Sweden is not on the Euro currency system. Some tourist shops do accept Euros or dollars, but this is the exception to the rule. Be prepared, if you wish to use cash, to have a supply of local currency with you.

> Cash is typically not needed.
>
> Using credit and debit cards is the norm here.

The official currency of Sweden is the Swedish Krona (SEK) and both paper and coins are in use. One mitigating factor here is this region is heavily geared to using credit cards, even local transit, so the need for local currency will not be great.

It can be daunting to see what appears to be a high price on almost everything as the exchange rate is slightly more than 10 krona per US Dollar or British Pound.

Currency exchange rates do change frequently but the following table may be of some help to guide you in what to expect when shopping and dining here.

Currency Exchange Rates as of April-2024			
(Subject to change)			
Currency	**100 Krona (SEK)**	**250 Krona**	**500 Krona**
Euro	€ 8.60	€ 21.48	€ 42.96
US Dollar	$ 9.16	$ 22.90	$ 45.80
British Pound	£ 7.40	£ 18.51	£ 37.02

You can easily exchange Euros or Dollars for Krona at the airport or at most larger airports in your home country.

~ ~ ~ ~ ~ ~

2: Traveling to Gothenburg

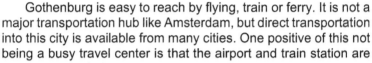

Gothenburg is easy to reach by flying, train or ferry. It is not a major transportation hub like Amsterdam, but direct transportation into this city is available from many cities. One positive of this not being a busy travel center is that the airport and train station are not overwhelming. Arriving by any mode of transportation is generally pleasurable and hassle-free.

Situated on Sweden's west coast, Gothenburg is central to major cities of Stockholm, Oslo, Malmö, and Copenhagen. It is also a direct ferry ride to northern Denmark.

Gothenburg Central Station
Photo source: Wikipedia

Should you choose to drive, this city and area are easy to navigate. Driving is on the right side of the road. The streets in and around Gothenburg are well laid out and there are multi-lane highways leading into and out of the city.

Trains and flights here are frequent and it is generally easy to obtain transportation which is convenient to your needs. If you are booking travel to and from here on your own, use trains if possible. The scenery along the way is beautiful and you can travel in a relaxed mode. Trains have an advantage of taking you into the heart of Gothenburg and the station is walking distance to many hotels and attractions.

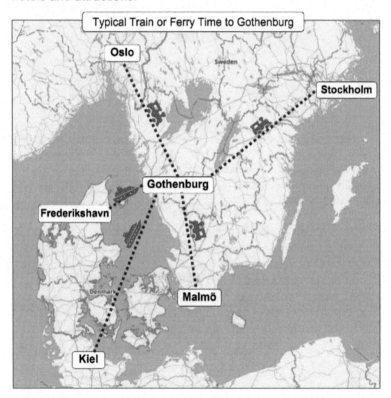

Typical Train or Ferry Time to Gothenburg

To/From	Mode of Travel	Avg Travel Time
Frederikshavn, Denmark	Ferry	3 Hours+
Kiel, Germany	Ferry	14 Hours
Malmö, Sweden	Train	3 Hours
Oslo, Norway	Train	3 ½ Hours
Stockholm, Sweden	Train	3 Hours+

Arriving by Train:

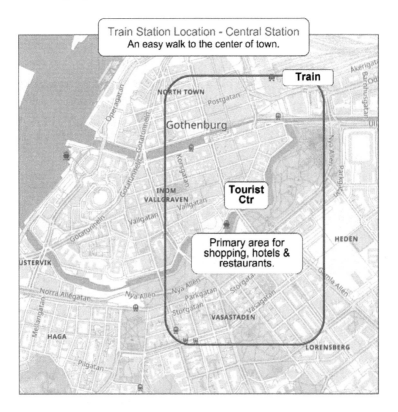

Train Station Location - Central Station
An easy walk to the center of town.

Trains are often the best way to travel to Gothenburg and you should be able to find direct trains from nearby cities. Most trains will have restrooms and food cars, but do not count on this.

Gothenburg has one primary train station, the Göteborg Central Station (Many signs site the station name as "Göteborg C"). This is unlike many larger cities which have several stations, causing you to take care as to which station you are utilizing. In Gothenburg, the station is well located and is only a short walk to the heart of the city and many hotels.

When you arrive in Gothenburg, you will find yourself in a mid-size station which is easy to navigate although it can be busy and crowded. It is the oldest active train station in Sweden which gives it a classical feel. It is also the second busiest station in Sweden with only Stockholm's main station being busier.

Inside the Göteborg Central Station
Photo Source: JIP-Wikimedia Commons

Upon exiting the station, you will come out to a big open square. Trams stop at the far side of the square should you choose to take one to your hotel or other destination. Taxis are also available.

Many larger hotels are located near the station. If you have chosen one of the following, you will have less than 2 blocks to walk to reach your destination for your stay: (See chapter 9 for further details on lodging.)

- Hotel Eggers
- Clarion Hotel Post and Hotel Odin
- Radisson Blu
- Scandia Europe Hotel
- First Hotel G

Booking Train Tickets. Booking train tickets in advance is easy and having a ticket in hand prior to your trip can be a stress-reliever. This is especially true in the summer months when tourist season is in swing. It is typically not necessary to book rail tickets for local trips in advance.

Several on-line websites are available which allow you to explore train schedules and make reservations. If possible, consider booking through the official train service's site SJ (www.SJ.SE). Using this site provides the advantage of being able to easily exchange tickets at the station at the last minute. Often, when booking through a third-party provider, exchanges or refunds must be made online or by mail and this process can be problematic if you have a late change in plans.

Other websites which provide train booking services online include: (but are not limited to):

- Rome2rio.com
- TheTrainLine.com

Arriving and Departing by Air:

Gothenburg's primary commercial airport, **Göteborg Landvetter Airport**[5], or GOT, is situated almost 16 miles southeast of the city center (distance varies by the route taken).

This is a mid-size airport and is not difficult to find your way from arrival gate and on through the terminal. If you are researching information on this airport, you may also find information on the "Gothenburg City Airport." This other airport is rarely used for commercial flights so little heed needs to be given to it.

Airport Hotels

If you have an early flight there are two hotels within walking distance of the terminal:

- Scandic Landvetter
- Landvetter Airport Hotel.

---

[5] Landvetter Airport Name: Gothenburg's main airport is in the town of Landvetter, thus the name "Gothenburg Landvetter Airport."

Travel time from the main airport generally takes between 20 to 30 minutes from the airport to the center of Gothenburg. No trains or tramlines service this airport. Your options for getting into town are:

- <u>Taxi/Uber</u> –This option, while the most expensive, offers the advantages of being taken directly to your hotel and is often the quickest. Taxis are readily available near the airport exit, so there is little need to book one in advance.

- <u>Bus</u> – Use the **FlyGBussarna.se** service. This bus departs approximately every 30 minutes and takes you to a depot directly across from the Gothenburg Visitor Centre. Note, when using this site, select the destination "Landvetter Airport" as the term Gothenburg airport is not used.

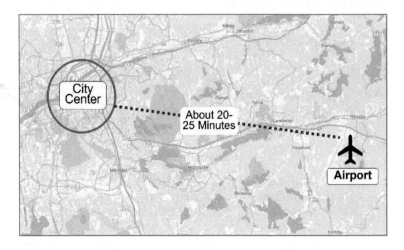

Details on the main Gothenburg airport, GOT, may be found at **www.GoteborgAirport.com**. This website provides helpful information on ground transportation and airport area hotels.

~ ~ ~ ~ ~ ~

Arriving or Departing by Ferry:

One of the most relaxing and enjoyable modes of travel to Gothenburg is by Ferry. Two major routes are available one across the North Sea from Denmark and the other, a much longer trip, comes from Germany.

StenaLine Ferry - **Gothenburg to Denmark & Germany**
Photo source: StenaLine

- From/To: Frederikshavn, Denmark. This ferry departs several times each day and typical travel time is around 3 ½ hours.

- From/To Kiel, Germany: This is a much longer trip, often overnight. The trip will take around 14 hours, but it does bring you much closer to the heart of Europe than traveling to Frederikshavn. This trip is infrequent with roughly one passage per day.

Booking Ferry Tickets: All travel on ferries is on StenaLine. For simplicity and ease of exchanging tickets, if the need arises, use the Stena Line website **www.StenaLineTravel.com**. Tickets may be acquired through other online booking services, but you lose some flexibility in exchanging or returning tickets when using them.

Ticket Types: All of Stena Line's ferries allow you to come on board either on foot or with an automobile, even an RV. When booking a trip which includes an auto, you will need to indicate the type and size of vehicle you will be traveling in.

When traveling from Kiel, you can book a private room. Given the 14-hour duration of this trip, having your own room can be advantageous. Several room types are available and full details, including 3D tours of each room classification may be found on the Stena Lines website.

Multiple Ferry Types

As a bit of a caution, Gothenburg also has a local ferry service with a terminal in a different area of town. When researching Gothenburg ferries, be sure to limit your search to Stena Line ferries.

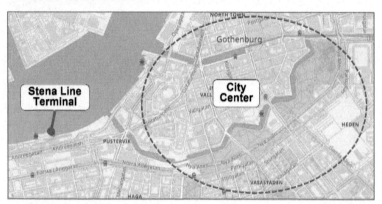

Getting to or from the Gothenburg Terminal: The ferry terminal in Gothenburg is near the city center, but it is advised to take available transportation to or from the terminal instead of walking.

It is roughly a 20-to-30-minute walk between the city center and the ferry terminal. Much of this walk is along busy streets which can be unappealing. Buses and trams are available, and both stop about 2 blocks from the ferry terminal. The tram and bus lines do not go directly to the ferry terminal. Within the Gothenburg ferry terminal, information is clearly posted on how to get to the tram lines.

3: When to Visit

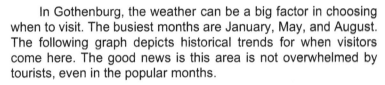

In Gothenburg, the weather can be a big factor in choosing when to visit. The busiest months are January, May, and August. The following graph depicts historical trends for when visitors come here. The good news is this area is not overwhelmed by tourists, even in the popular months.

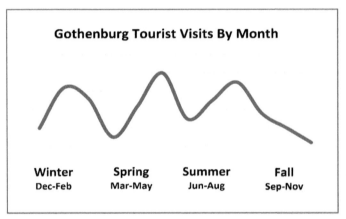

Gothenburg Tourist Visits By Month

| **Winter** | **Spring** | **Summer** | **Fall** |
| Dec-Feb | Mar-May | Jun-Aug | Sep-Nov |

Larger known cities such as Oslo, Copenhagen, and Stockholm receive far more tourist traffic.

As a general rule, when visiting in the more popular months, you will find higher prices for lodging and the need to make advance reservations for tours, transportation, and hotels increases.

One humorous saying in Sweden regarding the weather:

"There is no bad weather... just bad clothes."

Some Seasonal Considerations:

Winter (Dec – Feb): This area can be cold and gray from the start of the year to late February. Thanks to the benefits of the Gulf Stream, winters are not as cold as found in Stockholm and other cities nearby. Snow is common, but not so much as to inhibit travel. Many tours and tourist activities will be closed at this time of year. On the positive side, hotel rates are low and tourist crowds are non-existent during January and February. If you enjoy winter sports, there are several cross-country skiing and ice-skating opportunities in the area. Do not attempt to visit the islands as most facilities will be closed.

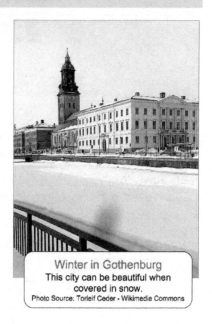

Winter in Gothenburg
This city can be beautiful when covered in snow.
Photo Source: Torleif Ceder - Wikimedia Commons

Spring (Mar-May): March will be much like February with cold and gray days and there is little tourism. A perfect time to venture out for winter activities as temps are better than in the dead of winter. By mid-April, tourism is starting to ramp up and tours which were not available in the winter start up again. Hotel rates, while not as low as winter, are generally good.

Summer (Jun-to-Aug): Summers in Gothenburg and the region can be beautiful. Your chances of being able to explore the city or nearby areas with favorable weather are high.

This is a perfect time to visit the islands or explore the coast and, if you visit, you will find many local individuals enjoying the islands as well for hiking or just sitting in the sun. On the downside, this is the most expensive time in the area for lodging. Every tour and tourist activity will be open which can greatly add to the fun you have when visiting.

Relaxing on the shore of one of the islands in the Archipelago in the summer.

Fall (Sep-Nov): Weather is generally pleasant with cool to warm temperatures. Rain chance is low in September and October. Most shops and tours will be open through October. Hotel rates decrease from their summer highs. All-in-all, probably the best time to visit here.

Typical Climate by Month				
Month		Avg High	Avg Low	Avg Precip.
Jan	😟	37 F / 3 C	29 F /-2 C	3.3 inches
Feb	😦	37 F / 3 C	29 F /-2 C	2.4 inches
Mar	😐	44 F /6 C	32 F /0 C	2.1 inches
Apr	😐	54 F /12 C	39 F /4 C	2 inches

Typical Climate by Month				
Month		Avg High	Avg Low	Avg Precip.
May	☺	63 F /17 C	47 F /8 C	2.1 inches
Jun	☺	68 F /20 C	54 F /12 C	2.1 inches
Jul	☺	73 F /23 C	58 F /15 C	2.9 inches
Aug	☺	71 F /22 C	57 F /14 C	3.7 inches
Sep	☺	64 F / 18 C	51 F /11 C	3.2 inches
Oct	😐	54 F /12 C	43 F /6 C	4 inches
Nov	😐	45 F /7 C	37 F / 3 C	3.3 inches
Dec	☹	40 F / 4 C	15 F / 0 C	3.4 inches

Major Festivals and Events in Gothenburg:

There are several popular events in and near Gothenburg each year. Visiting one of these can be a great addition to a tour of the area especially as many of the events put the area's culture and cuisine on display. The only moderate downsides are the added crowds and increased lodging rates for major events. Information on some of the leading events which have broad appeal follow.

The website **www.Goteborg.com** provides a comprehensive list of events, concerts, and festivals around the city and area. Details on location and timing are provided along with the ability to purchase tickets.

Winter:

- Christmas Markets – there are several Christmas markets in and around Gothenburg. The largest is held in the Liseberg Amusement Park. These markets run from late November to the end of the year.

Gothenburg Christmas Market at Liseberg Park

- Lucia Day (Saint Lucy)– celebrated every year on December 13. The practice of many Swedes is to go to churches or performance venues to view the traditional Lucia-train, an event where children dress in traditional wear and sing songs.

- Göteborg Film Festival. The largest film festival in Scandinavia. This runs for 10 days starting late in January and into February.

- Gothenburg Boat Show: If you enjoy yachts and boating, visit this show which is held in February each year.

Spring/Summer:

- Nordic Folk Alliance A two-day festival in late March focused on folk music and the music business.

- Walpurgus Night: Late April. A festival honoring Saint Valborg celebrated by large bon fines.

- Summer Burst: A large music festival which attracts well-known artists. Held each year in early June.

- Swedish Midsummer: Held in June on the day of the Summer Solstice. This is one of the most important holidays in

Scandinavia. Many shops and restaurants are closed for this holiday, so plan ahead.

- Gothenburg Cultural Festival: Held in late August to early September. An array of activities for children and adults including numerous events and shows which are held throughout the city. Check out **www.Goteborgskulturkalas.se** for details.

Fall Festivals:

- Göteborg Book Fair: Late September. A large and popular event spread across three days where noted authors and publishers are present for recent publications and literature. The website for this event is **www.Bokmassan.se.**

- Gothenburg International Science Festival: Late October to early November. One of Europe and Scandinavia's most popular science events which blends science with culture.

~ ~ ~ ~ ~ ~

4: Getting Around in Gothenburg

Walking, Trams, Hop-On Bus, and Boats

Gothenburg's historic and city center is easy to navigate and many of the leading attractions are near one another. Rental cars are rarely needed and most of your explorations may be done by walking or taking one of the convenient trams, or the Hop-on/Hop-Off buses. One of the few times you may want to take a taxi would be to travel to or from the airport or to neighboring towns for day trips.

Walking:

Most visitors stay in the area between the train station or near the canals. (See chapter 9 on where to stay in Gothenburg). By staying in this central area almost every leading attraction can be reached by a short, pleasant walk.

If you are in the mood to shop, the **Avenyn**, is a noted shopping street which stretches a kilometer in length, ending at the Museum of Art. All along this stretch are many shops, parks, and restaurants. At one end is the Visitor Centre which is a good central point to use for excursions. There are several side streets leading off from the Avenyn which are safe and have additional restaurants and shops to discover. A good place to start is Kungsportsavenyen, which leads you to the university and a park-like setting.

The map on the following page provides an overview of normal walking times within this area.

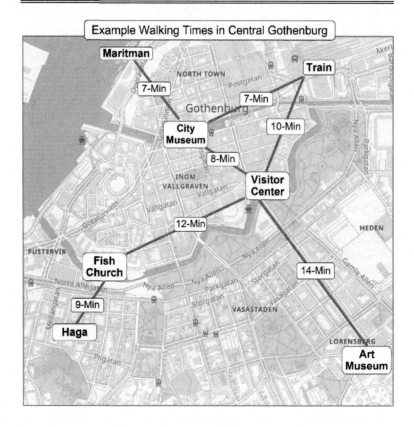

Example Walking Times in Central Gothenburg

Attractions Not Recommended to Walk to: Three attractions are NOT easy to reach on foot, primarily due to their distance from the center of the city. In each case, trams and/or the hop-on bus system will take you to them.

- Liseberg Amusement Park
- Botanical Garden
- Slottsskogen Park

Phone App: Strongly recommended to download is the "Gothenburg Map and Walks" app. This provides exact distances between locations, suggested tours, and many more helpful details.

Hop-On/Hop-Off Bus and Boat Tours:

Hop-On/Hop-Off bus tours can be found in most cities. In Gothenburg, there is the added attraction of Hop-On Boats. It is easy to think of this service as excessively touristy, but these bus and boat tours do offer several benefits.

In Gothenburg, several attractions are not within easy walking distance. Often it is easy to walk right by buildings or plazas with historical significance without knowing what you are missing. These tour buses will take you to most leading points of interest, including several such as the Haga historical area and Liseberg amusement park.

> **Availability Caution**
>
> The popular hop on bus tour may not be available for part or all of 2024. Check the website to determine current operating status.

The Hop-On bus makes eight stops around the city. You are allowed to get on or off as many times as you wish during the period of time your pass covers.

Gothenburg Hop-On/Hop-Off Bus
Photo source: Hop-On-Hop-Off-Bus-Tours.com

<u>Bus Tour Stops:</u> Attractions in the one-hour bus route include:

- Avenyn Street – the major shopping street in Gothenburg
- Feskekôrka – fish market
- Lilla Bommen – ferry terminal
- Opera House – this is situated near the art museum.
- City Gardens – large park in the center of the city
- Nordstan Shopping Center – large indoor mall
- Museum of Natural History and Slottsskogen Park
- Maritiman, Maritime Museum.

<u>Boat Tours:</u> The hop-on boat tours make a limited number of stops. Their chief attraction is the ability to cruise the river and canals for views of the city from a unique perspective. Most of the stops are within or adjacent to the historical center. Stops include:

- Feskekôrka – fish market
- Lilla Bommen ferry port
- City Center at Kungsportsplatsen
- Gothenburg City Museum

An additional two-hour offering, the **Padden Boat Tour**, takes visitors from central Gothenburg up the great harbor canal. This boat tour allows visitors to view numerous canal-side homes and lush natural areas.

<u>Frequency:</u>

- Buses run every 30 minutes during high season from May through September.
- Boat tours run approximately one per hour during the months of July through August.

~ ~ ~ ~ ~ ~

Trams and Buses:

The good and bad news on Gothenburg's tram network... it is extensive.

Good: you can easily travel to just about anywhere in the city on the trams.

Bad: It is so extensive that learning the system can be daunting to a first-time visitor. Using an app to help guide you is highly recommended.

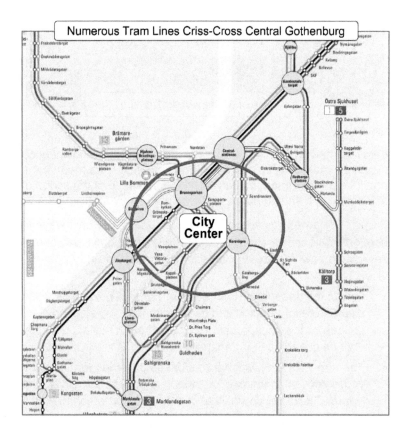

Numerous Tram Lines Criss-Cross Central Gothenburg

Gothenburg's tramway network is the largest in northern Europe. The system is comprised of almost 100 miles of track and is used by nearly 200 trams.

One of Gothenburg's Trams

The tram system has 12 different lines with over 130 stops. A detailed map of the system is not depicted in this guidebook simply because it is so extensive and complex. (The map on the previous page is intended only to provide a sense of the scope of this network. It should not be used for planning your tram trips.)

Apps: For a newcomer to Gothenburg, one of the best ways to comfortably learn the transportation system is to download one of several apps which are available for both Android and Apple devices.

- One of the better apps is **Västtrafik To Go**. This app provides exact route information and detailed maps. You also may buy passes for the transportation system through this app and use your device to pay for transportation.

- The app will detail which trams/buses or ferries to take once you select your starting or stopping points. To assist, the **Västtrafik to Go app** utilizes a map function which makes it easy to select your way points.

Ticket Purchase: Many options for obtaining tickets are available, including:

- Gothenburg Transportation Website and app: Visit **Vasttrafik.se** to purchase tickets for the trams and most other public transportation, including ferries.

  Tickets are available for a single trip, or for a full 24 or 72 hours. When purchasing a ticket for 24 or 72-hours, this includes unlimited travel on trams, ferries, or buses.

- Ticket Offices: Numerous locations throughout Gothenburg sell transportation passes. To find a location, ask at your hotel or visit **Vasstraffik.se** to view a list of locations. Ticket agencies include a variety of formal ticket offices and numerous sales outlets, such as drug stores, where tickets can be purchased.

- Purchase on Board: Credit Card Only. Single trip tickets may be purchased from kiosks found on trams and southern archipelago ferries. Bus tickets must be purchased in advance.

How to Use Tickets/Passes: In almost all cases, there will be either a card reader/scanner as you enter or, in some cases, you will need to show your pass to the driver. When using the card reader, simply have the machine read your card (or code on your phone app as you enter). Failing to do so can result in a fine.

Bicycle Rental:

Gothenburg is a great city to explore by bicycle and the local bike share system is excellent and convenient. Consider taking a bike ride along broad avenues from the heart of town out to the expansive Slottsskogen Park or neighboring Botanical Garden.

Download the **Next Bike app** to use for easy bike renting in Gothenburg and 200 cities worldwide.

Several firms provide bike rentals, and many provide services such as delivering bicycles directly to your lodging. The largest, and most affordable service is provided by Styr & Ställ which is operated by Next Bike, a large multi-nation bike-share service.[6]

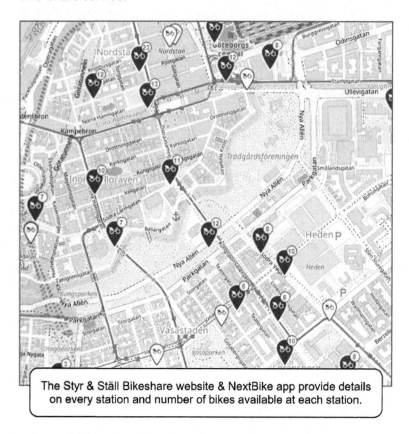

The Styr & Ställ Bikeshare website & NextBike app provide details on every station and number of bikes available at each station.

With the Styr & Ställ program, there are dozens of stations city-wide. You need to first establish an account with them either through the website, the app or at kiosks in Gothenburg. When

---

[6] Next Bike vs Stry and Ställ: This dual identity between Next Bike and Stry and Ställ can be confusing at first. If you are using an app, download NextBike and then select Gothenburg. If you wish to view the website, you will need to go to the Stry site cited in this chapter.

renting, you go to a station, select up to four bikes for one trip, provide your account information, and then return them to any station with open slots when you are done. You

are not required to return them to the station where you picked up the bike.

A Bike Share Station in Gothenburg
Photo source:W. Bulach - Wikimedia Commons

E-bikes are not available as of this writing in Gothenburg, but this firm does have E-bikes in several cities, and it is likely this option will be added.

~ ~ ~ ~ ~ ~

If you will be staying in Gothenburg and devoting multiple days to activities or tours in this city, you should consider purchasing one of the available passes should be considered.

Two different visitor passes are offered,the **Gothenburg Go City Pass** which provides a broad array of discounts, and the **Gothenburg Museum Card** which, as the name implies, is specific to some of the city's museums.

The Gothenburg Go City Pass:

This pass includes a comprehensive mix benefits. Similar to other city passes, it includes free access to area attractions along with discounts on many other destinations, including some guided tours

The **Gothenburg Go City Pass** provides value and convenience **IF** you plan on visiting multiple museums or similar attractions. They are fairly expensive, so do not purchase one if you are spending your time outside of the city, exploring parks, or just shopping and strolling.

The passes may be purchased online from **GoCity,** a firm which provides similar discount passes for several cities. As of this writing, the visitor center is no longer offering this product directly, but it is worth checking as, until recently, they had their own Gothenburg City Pass which was sponsored by Stroma. To order the pass directly, go to **www.GothenburgPass.com** (This takes you to GoCity.com's page for Gothenburg). You will first be guided to download the "**Go City" app** and, from there, select Gothenburg. One advantage of this program is you can add on other cities in the region such as Amsterdam and Stockholm.

As this is purchased and down-loaded online, the passes are available for use immediately. There is no paper version of this pass as of mid-2023.

When purchasing online you will be given the option of having the passes mailed to you or picking them up at the Visitor Centre.

Allow two weeks for the passes to be mailed to you once you purchase them online.

> Available in Other Cities as Well.
>
> The Go City Pass is available many other cities. Some areas within this region include Amsterdam and Stockholm.

Prices: Prices do vary so it is best to check online. As a rough guideline, as of April-2024, prices for an adult will be around those cited below:

- 1 day pass: Adult = 419 SEK / Child = 349 SEK. [7]
- 2-day pass: Adult = 544 SEK / Child = 419 SEK.
- 3-day pass: Adult = 614 SEK / Child = 464 SEK
- 5-day pass: Adult = 719 SEK / Child = 519 SEK

---

[7] Currency Conversion: As cited elsewhere in this guide, the Swedish Krona (SEK) can seem overly expensive due to the high numbers. In actuality, the prices aren't bad. A very, very rough conversion for Dollars, Euros or Pounds would put the exchange rate around 12 to 1, meaning that a 400 SEK item would be in the rough ballpark of 35 Pounds/Euros/Dollars.

Some of What Is Included in the Go City Pass:[8]

Transportation:

- Use of the Hop-On/Hop-Off Bus for 1 day. (Currently not running)
- NO use of local transportation such as trams, ferry or bus service. A separate Gothenburg transportation pass is suggested to use the trams, buses, and ferries.

Museums and Major Attractions: Free admission to numerous attractions including (and not limited to):

- Bohus Fortress
- Maritiman - ship museum
- Gothenburg City Museum
- Gothenburg Lookout
- Gothenburg Museum of Art
- Volvo Museum
- Tramway Museum
- Gunnebo House

The Tramway Museum is included in the Go City Pass.

Tours: Free admission to several area tours including:

- Padden Boat Tour
- Southern archipelago tour with guide
- Hop-On/Hop-Off bus and boat tours.
- Guided tour to Vinga island.

---

[8] Gothenburg Go City Pass Inclusions: This guide depicts many of the more notable sights included within the Gothenburg Pass. Not all tours and attractions are shown here as the list can and does change. Check **www.GothenburgPass.com** for an updated list.

Gothenburg Museum Card:

If your focus is on museums in around Gothenburg, another pass is available which is limited to the area museums. Unlike the main Gothenburg Pass which covers only a day or two, this pass, once purchased, is good for a full year and unlimited visits to each of the museums. This pass is intended more for local residents than visitors but is still available.

It covers the following museums in Gothenburg:
- Gothenburg Art Museum
- Museum of Gothenburg (City Museum)
- Maritime Museum
- Aquarium
- Röhsska Museum

Where to purchase and cost: The best way to acquire this pass is at any of the museums which it covers. It is available online, but an added service is involved. The cost, as of April-2024 is 140 SEK for adults and 120 SEK for seniors.

Gothenburg City and Area Tours & Providers:

If your schedule allows, consider taking one of the many available tours. These structured tours range from short 1-or-2-hour events to full day explorations.

Even if you are disinclined to join structured group events, at least one tour should be considered as they almost always enhance your understanding of the city, its history, and main attractions.

Many services offer and resell passes to the more popular

tours. Most tours of interest will be available from the Visitor Center, and many may be purchased in advance.

Numerous online services enable you to explore available tours and purchase passes.

These offerings often go well beyond those offered by the Visitor Center and some tours may be customized to your specifications.

This guidebook does not outline specific tours as there are so many great options for every type of tour matching a wide variety of interest groups. Following is a list of some of the more prominent tour providers and, from here, it is easy to structure a tour itinerary which fits your preferences.

Some of the Leading Tour Providers are:

- Go:teborg **– www.Goteborg.com**- The city's tourist website offers several walking and bus tours which can greatly appreciate your knowledge of this city and its history.

- Stromma **– www.Stromma.com** – this company serves Gothenburg and other cities in the area. Many of the tours marketed by other firms are provided by Stromma. A good site to view a broad array of tour offerings including boat excursions and even restaurant cruises.

- Goteborg Walking Tours **– www.GoteborgWalkingTours.com.**
Free and paid tours which take you to popular highlights such as the Haga district, the southern archipelago, and the fish market. (Many tours are free, but tips are suggested). Paid tours include photography and local cuisine explorations.

Swedish Fika
Consider one of the many walking & food tours of old town Gothenburg. Your tastebuds will thank you.

- Tours By Locals **– www.ToursByLocals.com/Gothenburg-Tours.** This firm provides tours to cities worldwide. Their tours tend to be personal with a private guide. Often, they will pick you up at your lodging. Many walking tours are available, including local shopping and cuisine tours.

- Gothenburg Tours – **www.GothenburgTours.se**. Private tours deemed "VIP Tours," which can be customized to your preferences. You determine the nature and length of tour, and how to be transported.

- Viator – **www.Viator.com** – a subsidiary of Trip Advisor. This firm provides a wide variety of tours ranging from private to large group. Like many online tour companies, they do not provide the tours themselves, but resell tours provided by local, often small, agencies.

- Lonely Planet – **www.LonelyPlanet.com/Sweden**. This world-wide provider of tours provides a wide array of tours which include several unique offerings. They are a well-rated firm.

The Ocean Bus
Looking for something different?
Consider a combined water and land tour of
Gothenburg on a floating bus.
www.OceanBus.se

~ ~ ~ ~ ~ ~

Gothenburg's city and historical center is fairly compact and is easy to explore much of this attractive city on foot. The area outlined by the canals has popular shopping streets, market halls, cafes, and attractions.

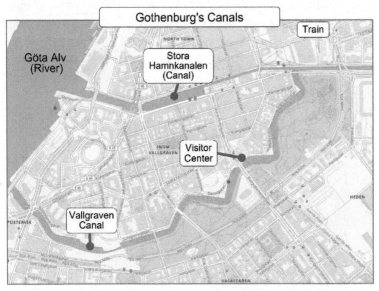

The large zigzag shaped canal, the Vallgraven, is referred to as a moat by many locals. This canal provides a pleasant dividing point in the town's layout. Alongside the canal there is a long park with shopping, the university, and businesses on the other side.

There are nearly 3,000 square feet of green space per citizen in Gothenburg. Parks, formal and informal, can be found both in the historical area and on the edge of town. In addition, an extensive network of bicycle paths run throughout the city.

When visiting Gothenburg, you will soon find that the streets are alive with pedestrians and bicyclists, even in the worst weather. There is an outdoor culture to Gothenburg and much of what this town is noted for is outdoor oriented. It is also a vibrant city where locals enjoy being outdoors, even in the cold winter months.

> **Explore the canals by boat.**
> Boat rentals are available along each of the major canals during high season. This can be a fun way to explore the city by winter and not just admire the canals from the streets above.

Points of Interest in Central Gothenburg:

The following is an overview of a variety of the city's attractions which include a variety of destinations such as historical plazas, museums, and even some notable shopping destinations. These are grouped geographically, and not by the type of destination.

The map on the following page highlights where each of these attractions are in town. Further location information is included with each description. In addition to these destinations, the following chapter lists several popular destinations which are still in Gothenburg but slightly outside of the city center.

Attractions In the City Center		
Map #	**Name**	**Nature of Attraction**
1	Maritiman	Ship and Boat Museum
2	City Museum / Göteborgs Stadsmuseum	History Museum
3	Christinae Church	Church

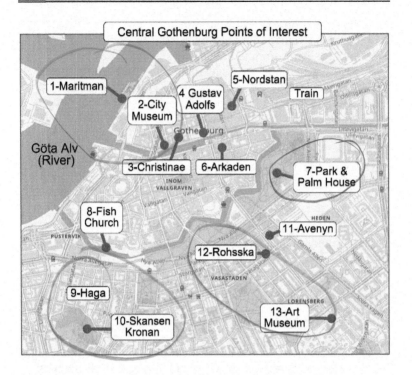

Central Gothenburg Points of Interest

Map #	Name	Nature of Attraction
4	Gustav Adolfs Torg	Plaza
5	Nordstan	Shopping Center
6	Arkaden	Shopping Center
7	Trädgårdsföreningen	Large park with palm house.
8	Feskekörka / Fish Church	Fish Market
9	Haga / Old Town	Historic Area
10	Skansen Kronan	Historic fort and city overlook

Map #	Name	Nature of Attraction
11	Avenyn / Kungsportsa-venyen	Shopping Street
12	Röhsska Museet	Design Museum
13	Gothenburg Art Museum	Art Museum

1 - Maritiman Museum:

This maritime museum has an impressive collection of boats and ships including a Swedish navy destroyer, a submarine, and several other vessels. It is an outdoor museum near the city center and situated on the river Göta älv. As of 2024, there are ten vessels on display and range from modern navy boats to historic ships such as the Sölve which was built in 1875.

Many of the vessels are open to tour, including the submarine, the HMS Nordkaparen. Every boat is on the water.

Maritiman Museum
A large collection of vessels to explore.
Photo source: Civilspanaren-Wikimedia Commons

In addition to the boats on the water, there are numerous exhibits throughout which provide interesting details and history on each vessel.

One enjoyable element of this museum is the café which is located on one of the boats, an historic ferry. This unique dining environment adds some fun to a visit.

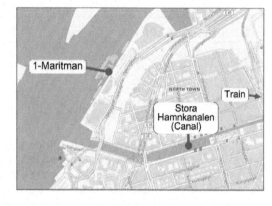

Location: Located on the river a few blocks north and west of the historic area.

- Walking: Approximately a 15-minute walk from the city center.

- Tram: The nearest tram stop at Lilla Bommen is only a 5-minute walk to this museum.

Hours: Varies by the season and day. Typically, the opening hours will be from 10AM to 5PM in the summer and shorter hours of 11AM to 4PM during the winter and spring. Check the website for the schedule which matches when you will be visiting.

Admission:
- Free if you have a Gothenburg Go City Pass.
- Rates vary by season with adult rates starting at 175 SEK and child rates at 110 SEK in the summer season. (Rates are as of April-2024 and subject to change)

Restaurant: A café is available for lunch or morning coffee.

Website: www.Maritiman.se

~ ~ ~ ~ ~ ~

2 - Gothenburg City Museum:

For starters, this expansive museum goes by multiple names. The Gothenburg City Museum or the Museum of Gothenburg. In Swedish, its name is Göteborgs Stadsmuseum.

Gothenburg City Museum / Museum of Gothenburg
Photo source: Wikimedia Commons

Located in what was once a warehouse for the Swedish East India Company, this building now houses a comprehensive history museum. There are exhibitions which portray the history of the area and of Gothenburg from prehistoric times to the industrial age. It is something of combination of: history museum, art museum and fashion museum.

Exhibits include relics from the Vikings, and you will find in-depth displays on the building of Gothenburg. For individuals interested in the area's involvement during WWII, you will find exhibits on this period of history.

Restaurant: As of this writing, the café is no longer open.

Hours: Open Tuesdays through Sunday. It opens at 10AM, but closing time varies by the day with the earliest closing time on the weekends at 5PM. Closed Monday[9]

Admission: (Credit card only – no cash)

- Free if you have a Gothenburg Go City Pass or Gothenburg Museum Card.
- Adults (without a pass) – 70 SEK (Subject to change).
- Free to anyone under 25.

Website: **GoteborgsStadsMuseum.Se**

Address: Norra Hamngatan 12, 411 14 Göteborg

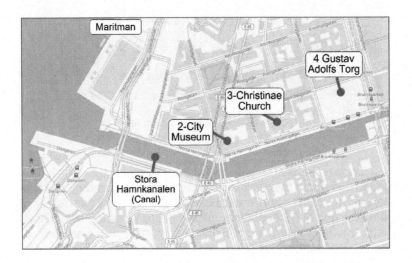

---

[9] Monday Museum Closures: Most museums are closed on Monday. Check each museum's schedule before visiting as exceptions may exist.

3 – Christinae Church / German Church:

Christinae Church / German Church

This is one of Gothenburg's iconic structures which, given its location along the canals and the tall belltower, makes for a perfect representation of the city. Built in 1748, this church was named after Queen Christiana, thus one of its names, the **Christinae Church**. It was used by the German and Dutch residents of Gothenburg giving it its other name, the **German Church**. The Swedish name is Christinenkirche.

This is now one of the city's most prominent Lutheran churches and, as such, is not generally open as a tourist destination. Visitors may come in to admire the interior and its many stained-glass windows. One of its great features is the bell tower which houses 42 bells. This bell carillon plays four times daily.

Hours: Closed on Monday. Hours vary by the day of the week. A good time to visit is typically from noon to 6PM.

Address: Norra Hamngatan 16, 411 14 Göteborg

Website: **www.Svenskakyrkan.se**

4 – Gustaf Adolfs torg:

Just a short walk from both the City Museum and the German Church is a pleasant plaza. The plaza is named after Gothenburg's founding father, Gustavas Adolphus, the king of Sweden in1854 when this square was renamed for him. In the center of the plaza is a statue of Gustavas.[10]   The statue is the oldest known public work of art in Gothenburg.

Gustav Adolfs torg
A prominent plaza in central Gothenburg

The plaza is bordered by prominent buildings including the city hall and the Bourse, a municipal building. This square is a popular spot for activities such as open markets and music events. During Christmas, the square is gaily decorated including a large Christmas tree.

Address: 417 66 Göteborg

---

[10] Not the only square in Sweden with this name. Some confusion can arise to travelers as prominent squares in Malmö and Stockholm have the same name.

5 & 6 – Two Shopping Centers– Nordstan and Arkaden:

Two popular indoor shopping centers may be found in the area near the main train station and also close to the Gustav Adolfs torg plaza.

These malls cater to locals so, with a few exceptions, this is not generally an area to find souvenirs. The historic Haga district is much better for that. If, however, you want a good array of Swedish stores for clothing, cosmetics and traditional gifts, these malls are great places to head to.

Nordstan Shopping Center: This center is surprisingly big and is one of the largest in Sweden. The complex houses 180 stores and is spread across several interconnecting buildings. If you are visiting by train, the center is connected to the train station by an underground tunnel.

Nordstan Shopping Center
Photo source: Torleif Ceder - Wikimedia Commons

This is a popular destination and the array of stores and restaurants is quite broad. It can get crowded, especially during the Christmas season.

Address: Götgatan 10, 411 05 Göteborg

Website: www.Nordstan.se

Arkaden Center: This indoor shopping area offers an interesting contrast to the huge Nordstan center. There are less than thirty shops here and there is a focus on fashion. It is, in general, a bit more upscale than Nordstan.

Address: Fredsgatan 1, 411 07 Göteborg

Website: www.ArkadenGalleria.se

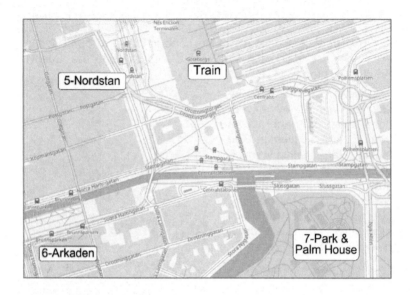

7 - Trädgärdsföreninger Park & Palm House:

The Palm House (Palmhuset)
One of several sights in Trädgädsföreninger Park

This large park is often cited as the "Garden Society of Gothenburg." It is essentially Gothenburg's central park and rests alongside a canal and next to the Avenyn, is often thought of as the cities prettiest. It is easy to reach on foot from almost anywhere in the city center. It is considered to be one of the best-preserved 19th century parks in Europe.

Established in 1842, this pleasant and peaceful place includes several historic buildings and gardens. During the summer, the large rose garden is a popular attraction.

Other buildings in the park include a well-preserved villa and the Rose Café.

During the summer, many concerts are held here on the large grassy areas.

Hours: Typical hours are from 7AM to 8PM

Address: Slussgatan 1, 411 06 Götenborg

Website: www.TradgardsForeningen.se

8 - Feskekôrka / Fish Church:

The "fish church" is a lively, indoor market specializing in fresh fish and shellfish. Come here to sample fish caught the same day and enjoy the great variety and displays and have a relaxing meal while here.

The building was opened in 1874 and the architecture was inspired by Scandinavian churches. When looking at the building, it is easy to see why many individuals first mistake it for a church.

> Closure Caution
>
> This popular fish market has been closed for extensive renovations. As of Jan 2024, a reopening date has not been announced.

It is built alongside the canal and is easy to reach on foot from the city center. In addition to the fish market, there are fish restaurants where you can also do take-away for an enjoyable day's picnic.

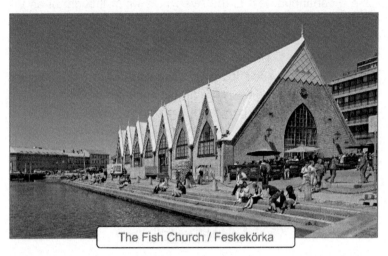

The Fish Church / Feskekörka

<u>Address</u>: Fisktorget 4, 411 20 Göteborg

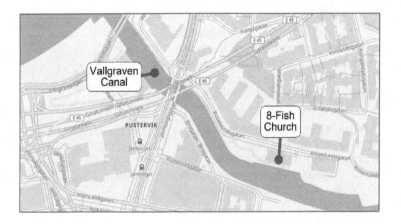

9 - Haga - Old City Center:

Haga - Old City District

Haga is a restored, historic section which is a popular spot for shopping, dining, and entertainment. This car-free neighborhood is lined with many preserved or restored houses. It is also a bit of a maze of narrow lanes which adds to the fun of exploring here.

This section of town is Gothenburg's first suburb. Built in the 17th century and was originally a working-class neighborhood. The name is derived from the Swedish word hage, which means enclosed field. In the 1980s, the area was largely rebuilt as it was run down and unwelcoming. Now, many of the buildings are new, built to match the older style as an area-wide renovation was completed in the 1980's.

The Hop-On/Hop-Off bus takes you to Haga. See chapter 4 for Hop-On bus details.

In addition to being a popular spot for visitors, it is an active residential neighborhood. At the heart of Haga is the street Haga

Nygata. This is where many of the shops may be found. This pedestrian street stretches from one end of Haga to the other, allowing visitors to fully experience much of the district.

Haga is a short walk from the city center, but you may also travel to here by tram. It is also close to the Skansen Kronan fort, so combining a visit to Haga with a visit to the fort is easy to do.

Tram Stops: Multiple tram lines service Haga with stops at the western and eastern sides. For specifics on which tram to take, either obtain a tram map from the Tourist Centre or utilize the Gothenburg "To Go" app which is available for Android and Apple devices.

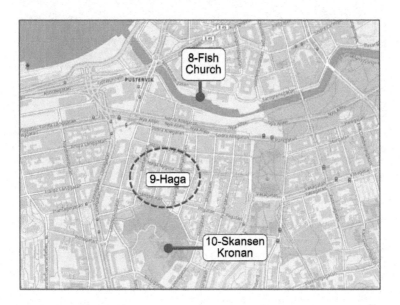

~ ~ ~ ~ ~ ~

10 - Skansen Kronan Fortress & Overlook:

Built in the 17th century, this fortress was designed to guard against possible Danish attack. It is one of a pair of such forts. The other is Skansen Lejonet, which sits on a bluff roughly 2.5 miles northeast of this position.

Skansen Kronan Fortress

Skansen Kronan fortress overlooks the historic Haga district. It is easy to combine a visit to this site with a stroll through the shops and restaurants in Haga.

When this impressive stone fortress was built, it had 23 canons and was a serious threat to any potential invader. It never was attacked or used in battle. Later in the 19th century, it became a prison. Later, during the 20th century, it was converted to a military museum which ran until 2004.

A visit to this location provides an impressive view over Gothenburg, the Haga district, and the river nearby. Tours are often conducted, and details may be found on the fort's website.

The Hop-On/Hop-Off bus takes you to stops near this fortress.

Many events such as weddings and conferences are held here, making it possible that the building may be closed to visitors when you come. The primary reasons to come here are for the view and for the sense of history which this structure provides.

Location: Located on a bluff overlooking the Haga district. It is roughly a 10-minute walk up to the fortress from the center of Haga if you choose to start from Haga.

Tram: If you are traveling from the city center, trams may be taken to the Göteborg Prinsgatan stop. A short, uphill trek is still required from where you depart the tram. Several lines stop here, so it is best to reference the tram map or app to determine the best route.

Facilities: Do not count on having access to restrooms when visiting here.

Website: **www.SkansenKronan.se.**

11 - Avenyn / Kungsportsavenyen:

The Avenyn / Kungsportsavenyen
Looking north from the Museum of Art

This broad avenue often simply referred to as "The Avenue" is a perfect place to start explorations. It runs for a kilometer through Gothenburg's city center. This important lane was established in the mid nineteenth century and is considered to be the heart of the city.

All along the way you will find restaurants, bars, and shops. Many of the restaurants have outdoor eating which can be enjoyable in the summer season. It is a busy place day and night and full of pedestrians, bicyclists, trams, and buses.

At the southern end, is the large Gothenburg Museum of Art. The northern end goes to the canals and Tourist Centre.

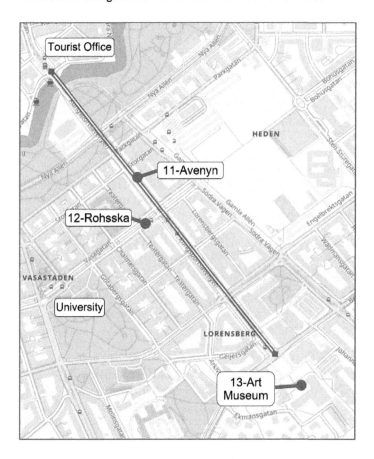

12 - Röhsska Museum / Röhsska Museet:

Gothenburg's Museum of Design and Craft is the only museum in Sweden oriented specifically to applied arts.

Situated near the popular Avenyn, this museum helps visitors understand how design is applied to everyday objects. There are displays ranging from prehistoric to current times. There are over 50,000 objects in the museum's collection.

Röhsska Museum Exterior
Photo source: H Sendelbach-Wikimedia Commons

Exhibits are updated frequently in addition to popular, long-standing displays. Check the museum's website to view the museum's schedule of temporary exhibits.

Location & Address: Situated on the prominent Vasagatan avenue, one block south-west of the Avenyn.

Vasagatan 39, 411 37 Göteborg

Hours: Normal hours are 11am to 5PM, Tuesday through Sunday. Closed on Monday. As with all museums in the area, hours are subject to change.

Admission:
- Free if you have a Gothenburg Go City Pass or Museum Pass
- 2024 adult rate is 70 SEK. Free if under 25.

Restaurant: A café is on site.

Website: **www.Rohsska.se**

13- Gothenburg Museum of Art:

Gothenburg Museum of Art
Photo source: Bolstermage - Wikipedia

Gothenburg's Museum of Art, the Göteborgs Konstmuseum, has one of the largest art collections in Northern Europe. Housed here are works from masters such as Rembrandt and Picasso along with many noted contemporary artists.

Among the impressive works found here is a large collection of Nordic art. This large Nordic gallery is one of the most popular sections of the museum.

Located at the southern end of Avenyn Kungsportsavenyen, one of Gothenburg's main thoroughfares, it is easy to reach on foot, tram, or bus. It is on a large square, the Götaplatsen, which has a

The museum includes works from noted artists such as Van Gogh and Monet

statue of Poseiden in the center. Also facing this square are the Contemporary Art Museum, the performing arts theater, and concert hall for Gothenburg's Symphony Orchestra.

> The Hop-On/Hop-Off bus takes you to this museum.

Hours: Tuesday and Thursday: 11AM to 6PM

- Wednesday: 11AM to 8PM
- Tuesday: 11AM to 6PM
- Friday – Saturday – Sunday: 11AM to 5PM
- Closed Monday

Admission:
- Free if you have a Gothenburg Go City Pass
- Adults (without a pass) – 70 SEK

Restaurant: A café is available for lunch or morning coffee.

Giftshop: A museum gift shop is near the main entry.

Website: www.GoteborgsSkonstMuseum.se

~ ~ ~ ~ ~ ~

In addition to the variety of sights in Gothenburg's city center which are outlined in the previous chapter, many interesting attractions sit just on the outskirts. Available to visitors is an array of places ranging from historical to kid-friendly amusement parks. Several of these are easily reached by the area's tram or ferry services.

Attractions outlined in this chapter include:

The popular island archipelago is listed separately and not included in this chapter. See chapter 8 for details on taking a day trip to the islands.

Attractions Just Outside of Central Gothenburg[11]		
Map #	Name	Distance from City Center
1	Liseberg Amusement Park	2.5 km / 1.5 mi
2	Slottsskogen City Park	4 km / 2.5 mi
3	Botanical Gardens	4 km / 2.5 mi
4	Gunnebo House / Gunnebo Slott	11 km / 6 mi

[11] Distances are measured from the Visitor's Center in central Gothenburg.

Attractions Just Outside of Central Gothenburg[11]		
Map #	Name	Distance from City Center
5	Aeroseum – Aviation Museum	17 km / 10 mi
6	Volvo Factory Visitors Center	14 km / 8 mi
7	Volvo Museum / World of Volvo	14 km / 8 mi
8	New Älvsborg Fortress	7.5 km / 4.5 mi

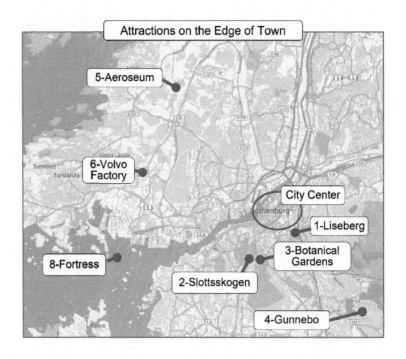

Attractions on the Edge of Town

~ ~ ~ ~ ~ ~

70

1 - Liseberg Amusement Park:

The most popular amusement park in Scandinavia, attracting three million visitors each year, is on the southern edge of the city center and easy to reach. The mix of rides and overall popularity ranks it of one of the top amusement parks in the world. Over three million people visit the park each year.

Gothenburg's largest Christmas market is held here each November through December.

This popular park first opened in 1923 and was a major feature of Gothenburg's 300-year anniversary.

Liseberg Amusement Park
Home to several large roller-coasters.

Rides range from an historic wooden rollercoaster to modern steel coasters. The array of rides is regularly evolving. One of the roller coasters, the *Balder,* has been named the best wooden rollercoaster in the world. Over 30 rides currently run during the high season and the rides and shows are designed to appeal people of all ages and there is a special area for young children.

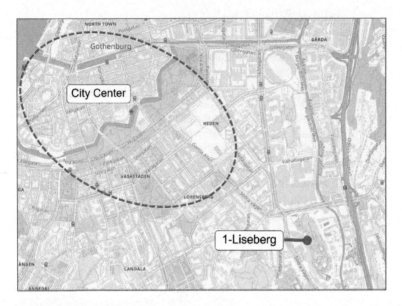

Getting Here: Trams are the easiest mode of travel for many individuals staying in Gothenburg's city center. The closest tram stop is Gothenburg-Korsvägen, which drops visitors off a short walk to the main park entrance.

If you have a Gothenburg Hop-On/Hop-Off pass, this tour bus stops at Liseberg and the neighboring Universeum, a popular science museum.

When Open: Primary season is late-Spring through Summer. It is also open for Halloween and the Christmas season.

Suggested Duration: Plan on staying for a minimum of 4 hours. Many individuals stay for a full day.

Website: www.Liseberg.com

~ ~ ~ ~ ~ ~

2 - Slottsskogen Park:

Two large and popular parks sit next to each other a short distance southwest from central Gothenburg. One of these, Slottsskogen Park is provides for a wonderful mix of activities which even includes the local zoo. Opened in 1874, this is a popular playground, even in the winter when locals come to cross-country ski.

The expansive Slottsskogen Park is a popular site for outdoor events.
Photo source: Andersreilund - Wikimedia Commons

Swedes have a love of the outdoors and this park with its mix of forest trails, open spaces, and formal/informal gardens is the perfect place to unwind.

What is Here: The park of over 330 acres offers visitors:
- Large open spaces for sports and children to play.
- A Segway center where you can rent and ride a Segway.
- Natural History Museum.
- Long, inviting forest trails to hike or jog.
- City zoo and children's zoo
- Multiple cafés

<u>Getting Here</u>: Slottsskogen Park is easy to reach via Tram. Take the tram to Linnéplatsen stop. An alternative is to get off at Botaniska Trädgården stop which provides access to the far end of the park and to the botanical garden.

<u>Website</u>: **www.Goteborg.se/slottsskogen**

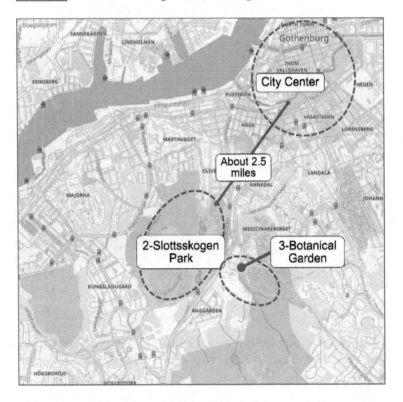

3 - Botanical Gardens / Botaniska & Nature Reserve:

Adjacent to Slotttsskogen park is the even larger Gothenburg Botanical Garden. This 430-acre (174 ha) facility is a mixture of formal gardens, the "Botaniska" aspect and a nature preserve with many hiking trails and ponds to explore.

The formal botanical garden was opened in 1923, along with other attractions such as Liseberg amusement park, to celebrate the city's 300th anniversary. Since opening, it has become Europe's largest botanical garden.

One of the many gardens to stroll through at Botaniska.
Photo source: A. Sheikh - Wikimedia Commons

Within the gardens there are There are over 16,000 species of plants presented in a variety of outdoor gardens and numerous greenhouses. The nature preserve provides a great opportunity to get deeply into nature without having to leave the city. The several trails take visitors through a variety of level forests and up to rocky promontories.

If you are here in the winter and enjoy cross-country skiing (Nordic skiing), this park provides a wonderful variety of ski trails ranging from open areas to forested and hilly areas.

Open all year, this is a great place to stroll the large grounds, get a coffee at the café, browse the garden shop, and visit the greenhouses. The highest spot is a lookout point which provides panoramic views of the city and the river. Sitting next to Slottsskogen park, the two parks combined can easily provide a full day of outdoor exploration.

An app is available which provides detailed maps and guidance on every aspect of the park. Use your app store to find the **"Botaniska App."**

Getting Here: Take the tram to the Botaniska Trädgården stop. This tram stop provides easy access to the botanical garden and the Slottsskogen park.

Address: Carl Skottsbergs Gata 22A, 413 19 Göteborg

Facilities: A café and restrooms are available in the park.

Websites: **www.Botaniska.se** & **www.Tradgardsresan.se**

4 - Gunnebo House and Gardens:

Gunnebo House & Gardens.
Photo source: Mkallgren - Wikimedia Commons

Located a few miles southeast of the city center is the **Gunnebo House** (often referred to as the Gunnebo Castle). This impressive mansion, built in the late 1700s, was once a summer home for a wealthy merchant. Today, it is a popular cultural landmark. One of the more notable features of this estate are the gardens, which are a mix of formal and free-flowing landscapes. The estate is situated on a hill between two lakes, providing delightful views.

Guided tours of the house and gardens are available all year and are provided in both English and Swedish. The tour of the house takes 45-minutes.

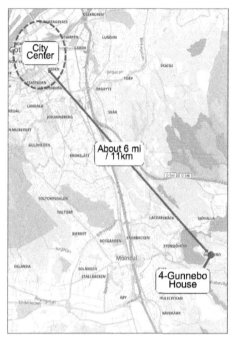

During the summer, concerts are held on the expansive lawns.

Getting Here: The estate is located in the town of Mölndal which is midway between the city center and the main airport. While it is situated out of town, it is easy to reach by a combination journey of train or tram and bus.

The journey typically takes about 30 minutes. Depending on your departure point in the city center, either a tram or train will take you here. Use the Gothenburg travel planner site Vasttrafik.se to determine the best route.

Facilities: A restaurant and bakery are available on the property.

Website: **www.Gunneboslott.se**

~ ~ ~ ~ ~ ~

5 - Aeroseum – Aviation Museum:

Interested in touring what was once a secret military bunker? This aviation museum is tucked away in an underground, cold-war, bunker which would be easy to miss if you didn't know it was there.

Aeroseum - Aviation Museum
A former secret military installation near Gothenburg

This is a large facility which sits next to an airport a few miles northwest of town. To first-time visitors, arriving here will feel unusual as there are few signs and no hint of the huge underground facility which sits inside a low hill.

The museum has many aircraft and other exhibits, much of which focuses on the Cold War. Exhibits include intriguing information on spying, the atomic bomb, and Sweden's Air Force.

In addition to the museum exhibits which are all in this underground bunker, there are fun and educational displays and even a flight simulator.

Getting Here: This is one of the more difficult attractions to reach if you do not have a car. When driving, it is a 17km drive (varies by route taken) of about 20 minutes. Taxis are not recommended due to the distance and wait involved.

Buses are available and a combination of buses from central Gothenburg will be necessary for most individuals. Bus 35 which departs from a station across the river from the city center, takes visitors to a stop which drops you off about a 10-minute walk to the Aeroseum.[12]

Hours: Open every day except holidays from 11AM to 6PM.

Address: Nya Bergets Väg 50, 417 47 Göteborg

Facilities: Restrooms and a café are on site.

Website: www.Aeroseum.se

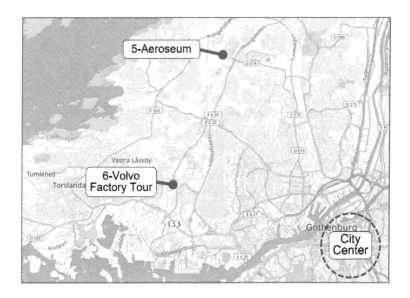

---

[12] Bus Route to Aeroseum: Use the website Vasttrrafik.se to plan bus and tram trips to the Aeroseum from central Gothenburg.

6 & 7– Volvo Factory Tours & Museum:

Auto enthusiasts can enjoy two different attractions provided by Volvo which is based in Gothenburg. They offer factory tours and a comprehensive museum. It is important to note that these two facilities are not in the same complex and each have their own hours, features and directions to get there.

Volvo Factory Tour: Volvo's main factory in Sweden is in the town of Torslanda, a suburb of Gothenburg. This factory is across the river and a bit north from the city center. Tours are offered including a full experience center. Full details on current hours and tour reservations may be found on the Volvo website.

Enjoy a group tour of the Volvo factory near Gothenburg

Website: Information on the factory tours is on the **www.VolvoCars.com** site but deeply buried. It is actually easier to just do a Google search for "Volvo Factory Tours Gothenberg."

Address: Huggasvägen 5, 405 31 Göteborg

Reservations: Booking in advance is recommended and cameras are not allowed. There is a fairly narrow time window for booking these tours as they typically do not come available until two or three months in advance.

Closed for one month each summer. The factory tours are generally not available from mid-July to mid-August each year due to factory-wide vacations.

Cost: The cost for these tours, as of Jan-2024 are Adults 200 SEK, Seniors 100 SEK. (Once you look at the currency conversion rates you will note that is not as painful as it first seems)

Volvo Museum / World of Volvo: This modern museum just relocated to a site near the Liseberg amusement park. So, given this move, do not try to visit the prior facility which was across the river.

This new facility is a mixture of museum and entertainment venue.

Location: Close to the Liseberg amusement park. The address is: Lyckholms Torg 1, Goteborg

Payment Note: The museum accepts credit cards or city passes only. Not cash.

Cost: Initial entry fees are 180 SEK for adults as of April 2024 and added fees for special exhibits and tours.

Website: **www.WorldofVolvo.com**

~ ~ ~ ~ ~ ~

8 - New Älvsborg Fortress / Nya Älvsborg:

This sea fortress, often referred to as Älvsborg Castle or New Älvsborg, is a well-preserved fort on a small island at the mouth of the Göta River. Built in the 1600s, it was made to protect Gothenburg from access via the North Sea. It was attacked during the early 1700s by the Danish and Norwegians without success.

Älvsborg Fortress
Situated on an island at the mouth of the Göta älv River
Photo Source: Wikimedia

The identity of this impressive fort is often confused with the original Old Älvsborg Fortress which is much closer to central Gothenburg.

This is one of the more popular excursions from Gothenburg. Visitors here may take guided tours or simply explore the grounds.

Another fort, Oscar II fortress, sits at the mouth of the bay near Älvsborg Fortress. Individuals desiring to explore more fortifications around Gothenburg will find this of interest. For information on this other fort, check: www.O2Fort.se.

Many individuals choose to stroll the perimeter walking paths with views of both the city and the sea.

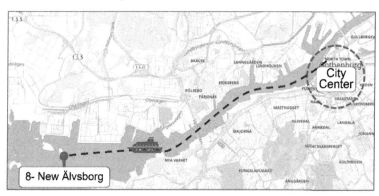

Getting Here: A boat trip of 30 minutes each way is required. During the ride, information about the fort is provided in Swedish and English. The boat departs from the Lilla Bommen ferry terminal which is close to the city center. It is a 10- to 15-minute walk to this terminal from the central rail station. There is no convenient tram stop, but 2 bus lines stop only one-block away.

Facilities: A café and restrooms are available on the island.

Website: www.AlvsborgsFastning.se

~ ~ ~ ~ ~

8: The Southern Archipelago

For many, spending a day exploring the islands off Sweden's west coast is at the top of the list of things to do outside of Gothenburg city center. The experience of catching a small ferry and doing some island hopping can be a joy. There is more than one grouping of islands, but the southern archipelago is the most popular and the easiest to travel to for first-time visitors.

One of the ferries which depart from the Saltholmen terminal for the archipelago.

Before heading out for a day or afternoon on the islands, it is important to understand the general nature of what is here.

These islands are not oriented around tourists, so do not go here expecting to find a cluster of gift shops or visitor-oriented activities. The islands have developed as a place for relaxed living and enjoyment of nature.

Photographers will find an array of photo-worthy subjects including the clusters of homes nestled throughout the islands, the rugged shoreline, and panoramic views.

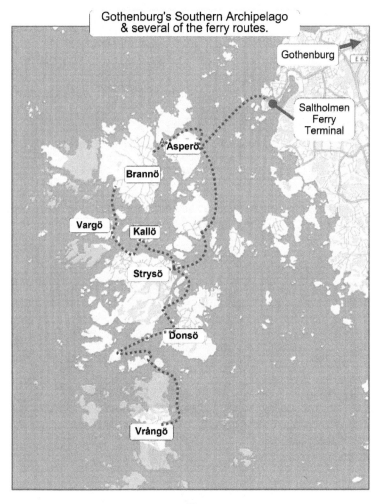

Gothenburg's Southern Archipelago & several of the ferry routes.

Gothenburg

Saltholmen Ferry Terminal

Åsperö

Brannö

Vargö

Kallö

Strysö

Donsö

Vrångö

The archipelego has many villages and rocky trails to explore such as the island of Styrsö.
Photo Source: Andrzej Otrebski - Wikimedia Commons

The larger islands such as Styrsö are well developed with many homes and small streets. When visiting the islands, it is common to stroll through narrow streets which are lined with small homes.

The islands in the southern archipelago are **mostly car-free**. Many residents of the islands do use golf carts, so be aware of them as you explore the islands. Bicycles may be

Relax at a cafe in the village of Bratten on the island of Styrsö.

rented but availability is limited.[13] You may bring a bicycle onto the ferry, but space is limited and can be problematic during peak summer periods.

Plan on walking or biking from most ferry stops. On occasion, you will find a restaurant and great views right at the dock, so a long hike is not necessary. It is important to have an understanding of the layout of each island. Maps are available online and at the ferry terminal in Saltholmen. Without this help, a visitor can find themselves taking a long walk to nowhere.

Some Helpful Island Travel Tips:

Getting to Saltholmen Ferry Terminal: This is a short ride by tram from central Gothenburg. The tram stops outside of the ferry terminal. Tram lines 11 and 13 come to this stop as well as bus lines 11E and 1140. Travel time from central Gothenburg is approximately 30 minutes depending on your starting point.

Ferry Routes: Several ferries depart Saltholmen, heading for different points in the island chain and even to the northern archipelago. This can be confusing if you do not have a destination in mind. Simply picking a random ferry stop is unwise as several of the ferry ports have little to offer a casual visitor. Most ferries depart at 1-hour intervals.

> **Guided boat tours** which cruise by the islands are available. (You do not get off of the tour boat).
>
> One such tour is included in the Gothenburg Pass.

Suggested Destinations: The following destinations have a variety of scenery, a café, and enjoyable walking opportunities: Styrsö Bratten, Styrsö Tången, Donsö & Vrangö. Most other stops do not have cafes or facilities for tourists. For your first ferry trip to the islands, consider selecting a ferry to one of these four stops.

---

[13] Bicycle Rental: The ferry stop at Styrsö Bratten is one of the better locations for renting a bicycle.

Tickets: Advance ticket purchase is not required. Day passes and the Gothenburg Travel Card covers not only the ferries, but the trams and buses as well. One purchase covers a full day of island hopping.

Website: www.VastsVerige.com/en. Details on provided on each route along with current schedules.

The village and port on Vrangö
Photo Source: Andrzej Otrebski - Wikimedia Commons

~ ~ ~ ~ ~ ~

9: Where to Stay in Gothenburg

Where you choose to stay when visiting a new city is essentially a personal choice. You may prefer hotels or rental apartments. Or picking a place guided by your budget may be critical to you.

Regardless of the motives which drive your selection or the type of accommodation you prefer, the "where in town should I stay?" question is critical to helping you have an enjoyable visit.

Budget and accommodation-type issues aside, the following criteria may be of importance to you:

- Convenience to historical sites, restaurants, shopping.
- Convenience to transportation.
- Noise levels around where you will stay.

> Recommendation:
>
> Stay near the Central Train Station. It provides easy access to transportation, museums and shopping.

While Gothenburg has lodging in almost every section of the city, for most visitors the choice is quite simple as there is just one area which provides everything you would want. This area is roughly defined as the sector between the Central Train Station and the Visitor Centre.

This guide does not provide details on all hotels in Gothenburg, there are simply too many to describe. There are many fine and dynamic online sources such as **Trip Advisor** or **Booking.com** which provide far more detail than can be provided here. These sites will provide answers to every question about a property which interests you and allow you to make reservations once you have made your selection.

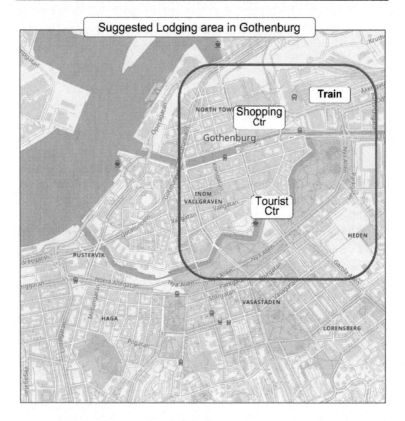

Benefits of staying in this area:

- Close to the central train station
- Near the river and canals
- Easy walking to ferry terminal
- Easy walking distance to many popular attractions
- Numerous restaurants and bars
- The Visitor Centre is here
- Several major tram and bus lines
- Nordstan shopping center and numerous small shops

Some Popular Lodging Spots to Consider:

Listed in the following pages are several of the more popular hotels to consider when coming to Gothenburg.[14] Each of the hotels listed here are well rated (minimum of 3.5 stars on leading hotel sites) and each has breakfast facilities. In almost every case, these properties are central to most visitors' needs and are likely

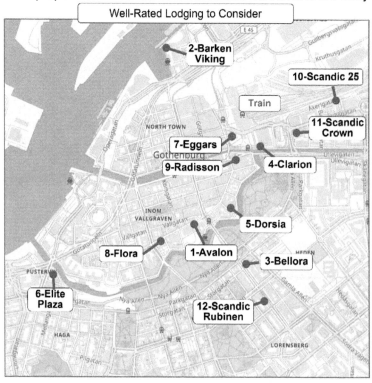

Well-Rated Lodging to Consider

2-Barken Viking
10-Scandic 25
Train
11-Scandic Crown
7-Eggars
9-Radisson
4-Clarion
5-Dorsia
8-Flora
1-Avalon
3-Bellora
6-Elite Plaza
12-Scandic Rubinen

---

[14] Apartments and Bed & Breakfast: This guide does not list these types of accommodations of which there are many in Gothenburg. If you prefer this type of lodging vs any of the hotels cited here, there are many excellent online resources to utilize to locate a place which fits your preferences.

to provide an enjoyable stay. These hotels are listed in alphabetical order and not in order of ranking by quality or any other element.

The Gothenburg Radisson Blu
Upscale hotel across from Central Station
Photo source: Tony Webster - Wikimedia Commons

Suggested Lodging in Central Gothenburg			
(All selected lodging has 3.5 or better rating)			
Map #	Hotel	Address & Website	Rating
1	Avalon Hotel	Kungstorget 9 411 17 Göteborg Modern hotel with full service and rooftop pool. www.AvalonHotel.se	4 stars
2	Barken	Lilla Bommens torg 10 411 04 Göteborg	3.5 stars

Suggested Lodging in Central Gothenburg			
(All selected lodging has 3.5 or better rating)			
Map #	Hotel	Address & Website	Rating
	Viking	This hotel is unique. Stay aboard a classic sailing ship. Rooms are cabins which provide a fun atmosphere. www.BarkenViking.net	
3	Bellora Hotel	Kungsportsavenyn 6 411 36 Göteborg Attractive boutique hotel on the popular Avenyn shopping street www.HotelBellora.se	4 stars
4	Clarion Hotel Post	Drottningtorget 10, 411 03 Göteborg Large, luxury hotel close to the rain station with views of a canal. Enjoy the rooftop pool. www.NordicChoiceHotels.com	4 stars
5	Dorsia Hotel & Restaurant	Trädgårdsgatan 6 411 08 Göteborg Very centrally located along the main canal and near the tourist center. Full-service, upscale property. A bit ornate. www.Dorsia.se	4 stars
6	Elite Plaza Hotel Gothenburg	Västra Hamngatan 3 404 22 Göteborg Large, upscale hotel short walk to train station or main shopping. www.Elite.se	4.5 stars

Suggested Lodging in Central Gothenburg

(All selected lodging has 3.5 or better rating)

Map #	Hotel	Address & Website	Rating
7	Hotel Eggers	Drottningtorget 2-4 411 03 Göteborg Across the street from the train station. Short walk to but a bit of a trek to museums and shopping. **www.HotelEggers.se**	4 stars
8	Hotel Flora	Grönsakstorget 2 411 07 Göteborg Boutique hotel which tends to cater to slightly younger crowd. The rooms are a bit small for some. **www.HotelFlora.se**	4 stars
9	Radisson Blu Scandinavian Hotel	Södra Hamngatan 59 401 24 Göteborg Close to the train station and canals. Easy walk to Avenyn and shopping. Large full-service property. **www.RadissonHotels.com**	4 stars
10	Scandic No 25	Burggrevegatan 25, 411 03 Göteborg Near the train station but a bit further from the center than other properties listed here. Overall, a good option for mid-range budgets. **www.ScandicHotels.com**	3.5 stars
11		Nils Ericsonsgatan 21 411 03 Göteborg	4 stars

Map #	Hotel	Address & Website	Rating
		Suggested Lodging in Central Gothenburg (All selected lodging has 3.5 or better rating)	
	Scandic Europa	Directly across from the train station. Large, modern property with a Scandinavian feel. Convenient to central Gothenburg. **www.ScandicHotels.se**	
12	Scandic Rubinen	Kungsportsavenyen 24 400 14 Göteborg This property is further south and away from the train station and canals than most other properties listed here. Next to the Avenyn for shopping and dining. High quality overall and the rooftop bar provides great views. **www.Elite.se**	4 stars

~ ~ ~ ~ ~ ~

10: Day Trips from Gothenburg

The leading day trip destination for many visitors will be the southern archipelago which was detailed in chapter 8 of this guide. A visit to these islands is a great adventure and provides wonderful opportunities for exploring, hiking, and photography. In addition to this island adventure, several opportunities for an enjoyable and active day out of town are available. These excursions from Gothenburg range from visits to the seaside villages, visits to historic forts, and enjoying the unlimited outdoor activities.

Cas are suggested for most of these trips.

If you have a car available while in Gothenburg, the options available to you expand greatly as the number of day trips which can conveniently be taken by train or bus are limited.

Road trips do not need to even have a specific destination such as the ones listed here. The scenery is attractive with unending forests and many lakes. Consider just hopping in your car and heading out to explore what Sweden is like. Head north or south along the beautiful and ragged coast or inland to the forest, farming and lake areas.

This chapter describes six popular places to visit, but this is far from the complete list of places to explore. All but one of the sites described here are all within a 90-minute drive of Gothenburg and offer a varied set of experiences. (The exception is Läckö Castle).

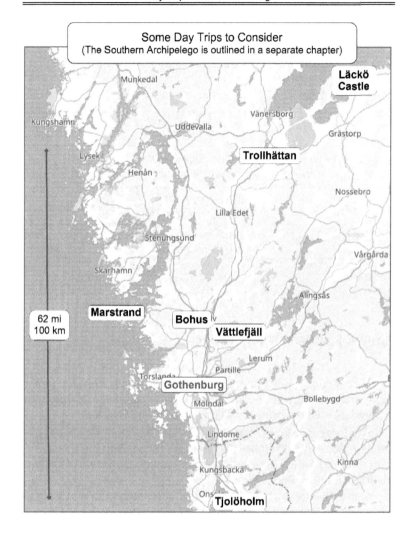

Some Day Trips to Consider
(The Southern Archipelego is outlined in a separate chapter)

The **rome2Rio** website and app is an excellent resource to use to help plan these trips and even book travel.

Recommended Day Trips from Gothenburg		
Location	Nature of Locale	Distance[15]
Bohus Fortress	700-year-old fort	20 km / 12 mi
Läckö Castle	Medieval Castle	158 km / 98 mi
Marstrand & Carlsten Fortress	Seaside village with fortress	48 km / 29 mi
Tjolöholm	19th century castle in beautiful setting	43 km / 26 mi
Trollhättan	Attractive town with SAAB museum.	76 km / 47 mi
Vättlefjäll	Nature preserve	34 km / 21 mi

Bohus Fortress / Bohus Fästning:

Established on an old border between Sweden and Norway, (the border has since changed), this fort was built over 700 years ago. It was attacked unsuccessfully many times by Norway and proved its value in protecting Gothenburg and Sweden.

The fortress is situated high on an island promontory overlooking the Göta älv and Nodre älv rivers. When visiting the ruins, you can explore most of the ancient fort and enjoy the views of the two rivers and the nearby village.

At the base of the fort, there is a large parking area and a small café with restrooms and the village of Kungälvs.

---

[15] Distances to Day Trip Destinations: All distances cited are measured from the Tourist Center in Gothenburg. When multiple viable routes are available, a rough average is cited.

Bohus Fortress

Location: The fortress is situated in Kungälvs 20 km (about 12 miles) north of Gothenburg.

How to Get Here: If you have a car, the drive is roughly 20 minutes from central Gothenburg.

Buses are available from central Gothenburg, and they stop at the base of the fortress. To determine the schedule, use the Västtrafik website or app. Travel time via bus is approximately 30 minutes, depending on your starting point within Gothenburg. If you have a Gothenburg Travel Pass, there is no additional fee to take the bus to here.

What Is Here: Once you arrive, there is a short uphill walk to the fort. Inside the fort, you are free to explore on your own. During high season, guides are often available with tours available in English. There is a trail which takes you around the

If you are driving to Bohus, it is easy to add in a trip to the seaside village of Marstrand.

base of the fort. On the walk, there are views of the rivers and a variety of flora to view.

Entrance fees: As of April-2024: Adults 120SEK, and Children: 60SEK. This is free if you have the Gothenburg Go City Pass.

Website: **www.BohusFastning.com**

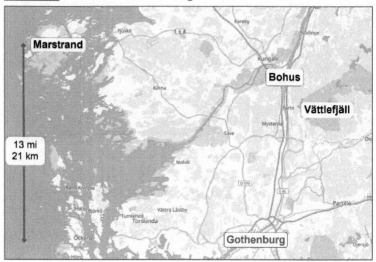

Marstrand Island and Carlsten Fortress:

Marstrand island has a bit of everything and is worth taking the 45-minute drive from Gothenburg.

- Beautiful seaside town
- Historic fort
- Car-free streets
- Sailing and boating activities
- Hiking trails to scenic spots on the island

Author Favorite
An absolutely charming destination with great scenery, a good variety of activities, shops and restaurants.

- Delightful restaurants and small shops to explore.

Marstrand - Sweden's Sailing Capital
with Carlsten Fortress overlooking the harbor.

Visiting here is a fun adventure for every member of the family. You first arrive on the island via a short ferry from the town of Marstrand. (Both areas have the designation of Marstrand). There is a large parking lot next to the passenger ferry (it does not take cars). From there, just walk onto the island and explore the town, the fortress, and everything the island has to offer.

A highlight of the island is the Carlsten Fortress. This complex with its commanding views of the island and harbor, was built in the 17th century. Tours are available or you can explore on your own.

How to Get Here: This island lies a short distance north of Gothenburg. It is easy to reach by car, bus, or a combination of train and bus. Travel time will range between 45-minutes to a little over an hour, depending on the mode of travel you choose.

Ferry Tickets: The ferry runs every 15 minutes during daytime hours. Advance reservations are not needed. Once you arrive, ticket machines are available to purchase ferry passes.

<u>Website:</u> For more details and information on this island and what to do here, view: **www.Marstrand.se**

Marstrand Port with Carlsten Fortress inn the background.
Photo source: Nick Sieger - Wikimedia Commons

Vättlefjäll Nature Preserve:

If you wish to get out of the city and into a nature area which offers diversity of scenery and activities, consider a day trip north to the large **Vättlefjäll Nature Preserve**. This expansive, and mostly undeveloped, area is one of the E.U.s network of protected areas.

- Over 6,300 acres of land and lakes to explore.
- Numerous hiking trails ranging in difficulty.
- Canoe rentals
- Swimming

- Rich forests and variety of wildlife

Vättlefjäll Nature Preserve
6,300+ acres of natural beauty.

How to Get Here: Located 20 to 30km north of Gothenburg (distance varies based on your destination within this large reserve), the best way to travel here is by car. Buses are available from Gothenburg, and they will take you as far as the town of Kryddnejlikegatan. From there, it is a 10-minute walk to the canoe rental center and the southern edge of this nature preserve.

Website: The site www.Naturkartan.se provides details on this and other parks and natural areas throughout Sweden. Given that many areas are covered in this site it is easiest to type in Vattlefjall, in the front page's search box. (The special characters in the name are not needed). Once you arrive at the section on the park, you will find extensive details on trails, facilities, directions and more.

~ ~ ~ ~ ~ ~

Läckö Castle / Läckö Slott [16]

This castle, one of Sweden's most popular tourist destinations, is the greatest distance from Gothenburg than other attractions listed here. You are rewarded for the distance involved as a visit to Läckö Castle will automatically include a visit to Lake Vänern and the town of Trollhättan.

Läckö Castle on Lake Vänern

Läckö Castle (also referred to as Läckö Slott) is a medieval castle which overlooks Lake Vänern. Building began in 1298, over 700 years ago. King Gustav Vasa of Sweden took possession in 1527 and held it as a summer residence.

---

[16] Travel Time Note: With travel time of roughly 2 hours each way, this is the only day trip outlined in this guide which is beyond 90-minutes each way. It is included due to the castle's popularity and the beauty of the area. It is a worthwhile day-long journey from Gothenburg with beautiful scenery along much of the way.

Today, the castle is a national monument which is open to tours of the interior and its numerous ornate rooms. In addition, visitors are encouraged to explore the beautiful grounds.

Location: The castle overlooks Lake Vänern on a peninsula of land which provides great views of **Sweden's largest lake** in many directions. It is in the village of Lidköping. This is 155km (roughly 96 miles) northeast of central Gothenburg.

How to Get Here: The best way to reach this castle is by car. It is approximately a 2-hour drive each way from central Gothenburg. Most of this drive is through open farm country and forested areas. Train and bus travel are available but, in each case, the one-way trip is over 4 hours. Trains take you only part way to the town of Lidköping with buses completing the final leg.

What Is Here: Tours of the castle are the prime attraction. For children, separate treasure-hunt tours are provided. During high season, English-language tours are provided every 30-minutes. During the summer months, be prepared to wait a while for an available tour.

In addition to tours of the castle, be sure to view the walled gardens if the weather allows. The gardens are used to supply the castle restaurant and adjoining hotel.

Cash is not accepted in the castle.
Be sure to bring credit cards with you.

Kayak and bike rentals are available in addition to several easy- to-hike trails.

Seasonal Note: The hours and tours available vary by the season. It is closed for much of the winter and tends to not open until April 1 for tours. Check the website listed below for operating hours which align when you will be visiting here.

Website: **www.LackoSlott.se**

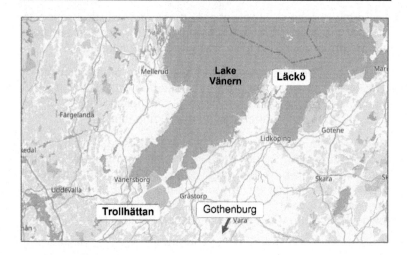

Trollhättan:

Trollhättan is a mid-size industrial city an hour northeast from Gothenburg. This is one of many towns in the area which make enjoyable daytrip destinations and it is easy to reach by car or train.

A visit here provides a look into Sweden's industrial development and history. Due to the location on the river Göta Älv and vast forestry reserves along with the Trollhättan Falls which powered local mills, the city grew into an important center of commerce. This is not a city designed for tourists, but it does provide visitors with several highlights.

Many of Sweden's film companies are based here, giving it the nickname of "Trollywood."

Consider combining a visit to Trollhättan with a trip to Lake Vänern. This will provide a good mix of nature, history, and city touring.

Among the notable businesses here was Saab. This auto and aircraft manufacturer were headquartered here. The large museum has over 70 historic vehicles on display.

- View www.SaabCarMuseum.se for details.

• The museum is near the river and central Trollhättan.

The Saab Museum in Trollhättan
Photo Source: Lukasz - Wikimedia Commons

Another popular activity is to view the waterfall and locks on the river. Watch as boats of all sizes work their way up or down river by navigating the large Trollhättan lock. This is a short walking distance from downtown.

How to Get Here: Numerous transportation options from Gothenburg to Trollhättan are available and the two cities are only 75km from each other. Trains and buses are readily available from central Gothenburg.

Driving is generally the best option. When visiting Trollhättan and this area, many of the sights are not close to each other. Having a car available reduces this problem.

If you choose to take the train and walk from there, the Saab Museum and the Trollhättan falls are a 25 to 30-minute walk.

~ ~ ~ ~ ~ ~

Tjolöholm Castle / Tjolöholms Slott:

A bit south from Gothenburg is a destination which provides visitors with an enjoyable combination of a beautiful mansion/castle, ornate gardens, trails, and beautiful coastal views. If you have access to a car, this is a very easy trip to do in a day or less.

Tjolöholm Castle
Photo Source: Wikimedia Commons

Built in 1904 on the expansive grounds of an estate which was held by a Scottish family since the 13th century. The castle was built as a country house and is largely done in a Tudor style. including Elizabethan and Art Nouveau. Tours are available and include access to a majority of the large building.

This estate is currently owned by the nearby town of Kungsbacka to be used as a recreational destination. Visitors to Tjolöloholm will find several enjoyable trails, and a shop and restaurant. It is a great place to have a picnic during the summer.

Tickets & Cost: Options of visiting with a guide or doing a self-guided tour are available and tickets may be purchased at the castle shop near the parking lot or purchase in advance from the website.

- Self-Guided: Adult is 150 SEK and 30 SEK for children.

- Guided Tour: Slightly higher fee for touring with a guide of 175 SEK for adult. During summer, these tours book up quickly and advance purchase via the website is advised.

How to Get Here: Travel by car is the best way to reach this site. It is an easy 40-minute drive along an excellent highway. The drive takes you through a variety of farms and forested area. There is a large parking area at the castle entrance and there is a fee for parking which varies depending on how long you are here.

An alternative mode of travel is to take a train-bus combination. The bus goes to the town of Frillesås which still is a nearly 1-hour walk to the castle entrance.

Website: **www.Tjoloholm.se.**

~ ~ ~ ~ ~ ~

Appendix: Helpful Online Resources

To help you expand your knowledge of this area, several online reference sites are listed in this appendix. Gothenburg and the surrounding area of Västra Götaland are popular places to visit, so this results in a wealth of material which may be of benefit in planning your trip.

Gothenburg City and Area Websites	
Each of these websites provides helpful information on the city, attractions, and events.	
Website Name	**Website Address & Description**
Go:teBorg	**www.Goteborg.com** The official visitor site and guide. Good information on almost every aspect of visiting this city and area.
Gothenburg Pass	**www.GothenburgPass.com** Details on the city card and provisions to purchase the cards online in advance of your trip.
Trip Advisor	**www.TripAdvisor.com** (Then search for Gothenburg) Detailed information, tour suggestions, and many reviews on hotels, tours, general city information, and more.

Gothenburg City and Area Websites

Each of these websites provides helpful information on the city, attractions, and events.

Website Name	Website Address & Description
This Is Gothenburg	**www.ThisIsGothenburg.com** Geared to individuals who enjoy getting out in the city and having an active nightlife. Information on upcoming events, restaurants, nightclubs, suggested walks, and much more.
The Crazy Tourist	**www.TheCrazyTourist.com** Then search for Gothenburg An enjoyable list of recommended 25 top things to do when visiting Gothenburg. Several helpful tips are included.
You Tube	Several helpful videos available. One of the best is under the search term "Places to see in Gothenburg."

Gothenburg Museums & Attractions

Attraction	Website
Go:teBorg	**www.Goteborg.com** This site provides an overview of the major museums and attractions in and near Gothenburg. Links to each museum are included. For almost any category of information, this site is a good place to start. Hotels, attractions, day trips, tours, restaurants, and much more.
Aeroseum Flight Museum	**www.Aeroseum.se** Information on the flight museum on the outskirts which is tucked away in a hidden cold war underground bunker.

Gothenburg Museums & Attractions

Attraction	Website
Gothenburg Botanical Garden	**www.Botaniska.se** Schedule of events, photo gallery, and details on this large botanical garden in Gothenburg.
Gothenburg Art Museum	**www.GoteborgSkonstMuseum.se** Details on this large museum including exhibit overviews, special events, and hours.
Gunnebo House	**www.Gunneboslott.se** Orientation to the Gunnebo House and Gardens including their restaurant and guest house. This historic mansion is just outside of central Gothenburg.
Liseberg Amusement Park	**www.Liseberg.com** Helpful information, maps, and ticket purchase for this popular amusement park.
Maritime Museum	**www.Maritiman.se** Details on this floating museum and the boats available to view. Information provided on the restaurant and menu.
Oscar II Fort	**www.o2Fort.se** Information, maps, and event information on the Oscar II fortress which is on the coast just west of central Gothenburg.

Gothenburg Museums & Attractions

Attraction	Website
Volvo Factory and Museum Tours	**www.VolvoCars.com** (Then search for factory tours) OR: **www.VolvoMuseum.com** Volvo has two different attractions in Gothenburg. Their factory and a museum. These are in different locations. This website provides helpful information on both.

Day Trip Destinations

Websites providing information on towns and locations you may want to explore outside of Gothenburg

Area	Website
Go:teborg	**www.Goteborg.com** Introductory information on locations to consider for day trips such as: - Southern archipelago - Vättlefjäll Nature Preserve - Gunnebo House - Bohus Fortress
Bohus Fortress	**www.BohusFastning.com** Helpful information on the historic Bohus Fortress which is an easy day trip from Gothenburg.
Lacko Castle	**www.LackoSlott.se** Details on the castle and adjoining hotel and restaurant which sit on Lake Vänern, Sweden's largest lake.

Day Trip Destinations

Websites providing information on towns and locations you may want to explore outside of Gothenburg

Area	Website
Vast Vierge	**www.Vastsverige.com** Information on visiting the Southern archipelago and other attractions along Sweden's west coast.
Marstrand Island and Fortress	**www.Marstrand.se** Details on Sweden's sailing capital including hiking trails and ticket information for the ferry and castle.
Saab Car Museum	**www.SaabCarMuseum.se** Information on the Saab auto museum in Trollhättan.

Transportation Information and Tickets

Website Name	Website
Gothenburg Pass	**www.GothenburgPass.com** Find guidance and ticket information on Gothenburg's Hop-On bus system.
Gothenburg Airport Transportation	**www.FlyGBussarna.se** Use this site to find and schedule transportation from the airport into central Gothenburg.
Swedish Rail	**www.Sj.se** Swedish rail site. View schedules and purchase tickets to/from Gothenburg.

Transportation Information and Tickets

Website Name	Website
Rome2rio	**www.Rome2rio.com** One of the best sites to view all transportation options for traveling to Gothenburg or heading out on day trips. Compare side-by-side info on buses, trains, cabs, and self-driving.
Västtrafik	**www.Vasttrafik.se** This is the best site to use for planning travel on Gothenburg's tram and bus system. Purchase tickets online. View all routes and stops.
Scandinavian Rail	**www.ScandinavianRail.com** Detailed information on the train system in Sweden, suggested train trips, rail passes, and ability to purchase passes online.
StenaLine Ferry	**www.StenaLine.nl**　　　　　　or **www.StenaLineTravel.com** Ferry schedules and reservations including travel to Gothenburg from Denmark and Germany.

Tour and Hotel Booking Sites

Websites which provide information on a variety of tour or hotel opportunities and enable you to make reservations online.

Company	Website
Hotel Sites	Numerous online sites enable you to review and book hotels online. Most of these sites also resell tours. - **Booking.com** - **Hotels.com**

Tour and Hotel Booking Sites

Websites which provide information on a variety of tour or hotel opportunities and enable you to make reservations online.

Company	Website
	- Expedia.com - Travelocity.com
Goteborg Walking Tours	**www.GoteborgWalkingTours.com** Details and reservations for several free and paid walking tours in central Gothenburg.
Tour Resellers	Many companies, such as the ones listed here, provide a full variety of tours to Gothenburg as well as day tours. The offerings are similar, but research is helpful as some firms offer unique services and tours. - **GetYourGuide.com** - **ToursByLocals.com** - **Viator.com** - **WorldTravelGuide.net** - **LonelyPlanet.com**
Trip Advisor	**www.TripAdvisor.com** One of the most comprehensive sites on hotels and tours. Direct connection with Viator, a tour reseller.

~ ~ ~ ~ ~

Index

o

www.StartingPointGuides.com

This guidebook on Gothenburg is one of several current and planned *Starting-Point Guides*. Each book in the series is developed with the concept of using one enjoyable city as your basecamp and then exploring from there.

Current guidebooks are for:

Austria:

- Salzburg, and the Salzburg area.

France:

- Bordeaux, Plus the surrounding Gironde River region
- Dijon Plus the Burgundy Region
- Lille and the Nord-Pas-de-Calais Area.
- Nantes and the western Loire Valley.
- Reims and Épernay the heart of the Champagne Region.
- Strasbourg, and the central Alsace region.
- Toulouse, and the Haute-Garonne area.

Germany:

- Cologne & Bonn
- Dresden and the Saxony State
- Stuttgart and the and the Baden-Württemberg area.

Spain:

- Camino Easy: A mature walker's guide to the popular Camino de Santiago trail.

- <u>Toledo:</u> The City of Three Cultures

Sweden:

- <u>Gothenburg</u> Plus the Västra Götaland region.

Switzerland:

- <u>Geneva</u>, Including the Lake Geneva area.
- <u>Lucerne</u>, Including the Lake Lucerne area.
- <u>Zurich </u>– And the Lake Zurich area.

Updates on these and other titles may be found on the author's Facebook page at:

www.Facebook.com/BGPreston.author

Feel free to use this Facebook page to provide feedback and suggestions to the author or email to: cincy3@gmail.com